Published by I AM WORDS
Copyright © 2011 by CM.SPENCE

ISBN –978-0-9834455-1-7
ISBN –978-0-9834455-1-7
First Printing April 2011
Printed in the United States of America
10 9 8 7 6 5 4 3 2 1

This is a work of fiction. It is not meant to depict, portray or represent any particular real persons. Names, characters, places, and incidents are either the product of the author's imagination or are used fictitiously, and any resemblance to actual persons living or dead, business establishments, events or locales is entirely coincidental.

Cover Design: Junnita Jackson/We Read Literary Services
Edited By: VaLonda Harris/ Dana Vincent
Proof Read By: Sammiyah Harvey, MaDonna Awotwi, Brandie Hill

I AM WORDS Publishing/2Writers Inc.
Po Box 2406
Harrisburg, Pa. 17105
www.cmspence.bigcartel.com
facebook.com/cmspencewrites

Giving honor to God, who is the head of my life .To the Pastor of this house of worship, deacons, saints and friends.... Ya'll know I'm silly! Seriously, there are several people who have made this dream possible. Thank you to: **To Charlie Mae Hill and Lucy Mae Spencer,** not only did I blend your names, but I pray I have taken on your spirit, tenacity, and femininity. You were two of the most God-fearing individuals in my life. Thank you for your example as Christians, as mothers, but most of all as virtuous women. **Freddie and Rhonda Hill**, who make me believe in true love. **Jennifer, Brandie, Lloyd, Ryan, Trenity, and DuShawn** for making me the proudest sister to walk the face of this Earth. **Tamia** for saving my life. **The entire Hill and Spencer families.** I love you all! **Leann Tepsich Cox**, thanks for believing in me in the 5th grade. I never forgot my promise to you! To "**My Dre**," you are and always will be my hip hop. I love you... "Your Sid." **Sankofa**, THE WORLD, Sis! Nothing less. **Tiger Rose**, you're a beast. I love you both. IAmWords! **Junnita Jackson**, for this beautiful cover and the inspiration to use my talent to provide. You're awesome. **Dana Vincent and VaLonda Harris.** Thank you for editing this book and your kind words! Ya'll ready for the next one? **Samiyyah Harvey**, WE DID IT! There's no possible way I could have done this without you. To The F.B.A.'s: **Giovanna Davis-Brown, Lakisha Goodman-Gaymon, Latasha Goodman-Shears, Mar L.N. Harper, Joy Matthews, and Deedra D. Vincent** your constant encouragement reminded me that I could do this, even when I forgot. Bob's! **Kristen Tate-Hamn**, thank you for making me feel like a star, for your love and support, and for sharing your first born with my first born. **To Rose "New York" Paul**, thank you for threatening bodily harm if I did not live up to my potential. I am grateful for your unconditional (yet scary) love. **Helen Wormsley, Gail Elliott-Tillery, Alexis C.P. Jones-Terry, and Mercedes L. Brown**, we've been friends so long, I can't really remember life without you all. I don't want to ever imagine it that way. **Toni Ware, Melody Fennell, and Jayme Madden**: "I plead the fifth." You all are always there when I need you most. To **Beth Dagenhart Greenwalt, LaQuashja Jones-Lowden** *most supportive woman I know*, **Demetrius Pinder, and April Jacobs**: your faith in me has humbled me more than you will ever know.

Finally, to "**Tamra**" thank you for showing me by example what it means to LIVE. Who would have thought that one phone conversation would turn into this? I know...we both did! Here's to long phone conversations, amazing road trips, laughing until our stomachs hurt, and a friendship that I will forever hold dear.

To anyone who has encouraged me, checked in on me, and supported this crazy dream of mine, thank you seems so shallow, but from the very bottom of my heart...I am eternally grateful.

All those who know a word of prayer, continue to pray my strength in the Lord!

Hugs and Love,
CM Spence

The Jacksons —

HOLY TRINITY

Thank you for
supporting my passion.

♡

M Spence

3/2021

Chapter 1

"Come to Jesus. Come to Jesus. Come to Jesus, just now." Tamra felt the choir was singing to her, but her feet felt like they had been nailed to the floor. Her heart raced with her mind in hot pursuit. The anxiety made her dizzy. She closed her eyes, fanned herself, and sang along hoping that someone else would walk down the aisle. The choir kept singing.

She heard whispers of thanks to God and Deaconess Tillery belt out a "Yes, Gawd!" from behind her. Wait! DeaconessTillery? She had been sitting two rows in front of Tamra. She opened her eyes. She was walking down the middle aisle. She was walking right through those invisible, open doors of the church without realizing she had ever gotten out of her seat.

Tamra had visited Bible Tabernacle two months earlier and immediately felt at home. It was exactly what she needed. The structure her mail was delivered to each day had become a living nightmare. It had stopped being home months ago.

It started the day Kya died. Had Tamra known what the months after her daughter's death would be like, she would have never buried her in William Howard Day Cemetery. She would have brought her cold remains to their house on Rudy Road. Certainly, it was as good of a tomb as any one the funeral director had shown her. But, Kya had gone on to a "better place." Apparently, she took her family's smiles with her. The color drained from their faces with each searing tear. The entire Jordan family was quickly fading to gray.

Pastor Givens hugged her tight and thumped her back so hard she thought she'd cough up a lung. He spun her around.

"I know we know you," he said with a raspy voice from preaching. "But, tell us your name so the church clerk can get you a welcome packet." He shoved the microphone in her face.

"Tamra Baker-Jordan." The church erupted.

"And who is this little cherub?" He bent down and gave her daughter a mouthful of microphone, too. "Jayla Skye Jordan!" Tamra's youngest daughter said proudly. The church went off again. *It don't take much for these folks to get happy*, Tamra thought to herself.

Pastor Givens rattled through a list of boards she could join and programs Jayla could participate in. Then he talked about a new members' class that she was to start attending. *Isn't that what service is for?*

This was all new to Tamra. She wasn't raised in the church. She came from a loving home with her father and stepmother who taught her that being a good person was all the religion she needed. She had heard whispers of them being wronged by their former church, but she learned not to ask questions about it.

Tamra wasn't quite sure why they called it the right hand of fellowship. Not one person shook her hand. They all grabbed her and hugged her enthusiastically before doing the same to Jayla, who was beaming from all this attention. Tamra made a mental note to read over her official welcome packet to see when the hugging class was held. She was sure they had one. And she'd bet that Pastor Givens was the teacher.

"Thank you, Jesus," she said aloud when she realized she had hugged the last person. The pastor echoed her statement. She held back a chuckle and tried not to visibly stretch her now aching arms. *This must be what Bernie Mac was talking about in Kings of Comedy!*

After what felt like an eternity, Tamra returned to her seat with her seven-year-old bopping right behind her. Service was dismissed shortly afterward. Her heart sank and her feet began to feel heavy. She hated when church ended. Members of the congregation came up to her, asking her stay for the meal in the fellowship hall.

"I'd love to but, we really must get going. We've got to get home," her voice trailed on the last word. By now, her chocolate brown suede pumps felt like someone had filled them with cement.

"Mommy!" Jayla protested. Tamra cut her eyes at her but deep down she wanted to stay just as badly as her daughter. Jayla took the hint and said no more.

Jayla's silence ended the moment her seatbelt clicked. She buzzed with excitement about joining church. She rummaged through the plastic bag she had been given and dropped the contents on the floor mat in front of her when the next item in the bag caught her eye.

"Mommy, I'm gonna join the children's choir. And can I usher with Imani?"

"Sure, Jayla," unsure of what she had just agreed to. Tamra's mind was elsewhere. She knew she had made the right decision today, even though she didn't recall actually making it. She had tried everything else to save herself. To save her sanity. She knew she needed a higher power.

Since she had acknowledged the presence of God, she began seeing Him all around her. He was in Jayla's smile. He was in the songs the birds sang that woke her up just before her alarm clock went off in the morning. He was nestled between each blade of grass that seemed to grow in unison on her neatly manicured block. But, just like she noticed God, she noticed the devil. He visited her in her thoughts. He dwelled in the dark, lonely hours of the night. He lived in her house.

Jayla and Tamra walked into the front door lightly. Chances were Joe Joe was in the basement. The commentator's voice blaring from the television indicated that he was. If Tamra could predict the Power Ball numbers like she could predict the whereabouts of her husband, she'd be filthy, stinkin' rich. She pushed the basement door open a crack and yelled down. "Joe Joe, we're home." She didn't even wait for the silence she knew would follow.

Tamra kicked her shoes off and started boiling a pot of water before deciding what she was about to cook. Jayla ran in the kitchen and stood in front of the refrigerator with the door wide open.

"Jay Jay, you already know what's in there. Can you pick something and shut the door?" Jayla grabbed a bottle of water and skipped into the living room. Tamra went over to the freezer, opened it and stared inside. Chicken, beef for spaghetti, steaks. She couldn't decide.

"Hey, Mommy. You know what's in there. Shut that door." Jayla teased. Tamra ran into the living room, jumped on the couch and began to tickle her daughter. She giggled and squealed with delight. Tamra loved to hear her laugh. It was the purest form of happiness. The more Jayla laughed in life, the less Tamra felt the urge to sob.

It wasn't just the death of Kya that weighed on Tamra. That was the devastating blow that left her hopeless, though. Life hadn't been perfect by any means prior to that. But, it was manageable. They had a mortgage, two car payments, and two rapidly sprouting crumb-snatchers that were growing faster than Tamra and Joe Joe could keep up with. Looking back on it, they had a home, transportation, and more love around their dining room table than some people experienced their whole lives. Sadly, it took tragic loss to identify all they had gained.

The sound of two ice cubes hitting the bottom of an empty glass seemed to pierce the air. It immediately silenced Tamra and Jayla's laughter. Sucked the air right out of the room. Tamra shot Jayla a look, warning her to stay put. Jayla looked like she was too scared to move even if she wanted to. Tamra quickly ran into the kitchen, her stocking feet barely hit the floor.

"Joe Joe…uh…sorry…" she stammered. "I didn't even hear you come up the steps."

"How was church?"

"Very nice. Jay Jay and I joined today." She waited for a reaction. He filled his glass to the brim and headed to the basement door. "I'll be downstairs," he said over his shoulder.

Tamra grabbed the edge of the kitchen counter and clutched it until her knuckles were almost white. She started to pray. She prayed for wisdom and clarity. She prayed for understanding. She asked why God had chosen to take her daughter and her husband away from her.

Tamra and Jayla ate dinner and enjoyed their Sunday night lineup. They laughed at America's Funniest Home Videos, cried at Extreme Home Makeover, and Tamra shooed Jayla to bed as Desperate Housewives came on. Soon it felt like cinderblocks had been tied to each of her eyelashes, so she went to bed.

She tossed and turned and couldn't get comfortable. She thought about when her bed used to be her haven. There were nights when she'd crawl under the covers and nearly fall asleep before her head hit the pillow. She was greeted by the arms that she fit into perfectly. She was sure that her life was a puzzle and it was complete. But, now it seemed that someone had taken their arm and swiped the pieces into countless different directions. Tamra had concluded that some pieces were gone forever. Some were just better left lying on the floor.

She watched television, tossed and turned some more, and then she watched the blades of the ceiling fan twirl until her eyes crossed. Sleep would not come. She sighed heavily and headed to the kitchen. Tamra decided to make herself a drink to help her slip into dreamland. Joe Joe had a vast array of things to choose from. *Just a sip*, she assured herself.

Trapped in her own thoughts, she didn't notice Joe Joe standing in front of the fireplace...sobbing. He was looking at the oversized portrait on the mantle. The four of them were smiling radiantly. The colors in their new Easter outfits seemed to pop off the canvass. Their love was tangible. He lightly caressed Kya's face on the picture. She wanted to run to him, comfort and console him, tell him everything would be alright. But, they were practically strangers now. She had no clue what to say to her own husband.

"Why'd she have to die, Tam?" Tamra was so used to him not speaking to her, it took a second for it to register that he really wanted her to answer.

"Joe Joe, God knows best."

"I don't need your holy rhetoric right now!" He turned to her in a rage. His eyes were wild with fury. "You're so busy being a saint. How about you try being my wife?" His speech was slurred. "She was your daughter, too. And she's dead...she's dead." His words trailed off into a whimper. His shoulders shook violently as his pain manifested in tears.

"Come to bed with me tonight, Joe Joe."

Tamra reluctantly walked to him. She nestled her face in his neck and inhaled. She missed his scent. She slowly turned to walk up the stairs and prayed he would actually follow her. He did. She grabbed his hand and interlocked her fingers with his.

Joe Joe laid on his side of the bed for the first time in forever. He held the covers up, indicating for Tamra to slip in with him. She looked at clothes that needed to be put away and thought about clothes that needed to be pulled out for the next day. Then she looked at her husband in the spot she had tirelessly prayed he'd return to. Those clothes could wait. He had needed her for far too long. He wrapped his arms around her and the sleepiness she was previously searching for immediately fell upon her. Tamra took one deep breath and began to drift off. She couldn't help but smile. No matter how long a puzzle piece is on the floor, when it's put back in the proper place, it seems it was never gone. Tamra and Joe Joe still fit.

Chapter 2

The sun burst through the master bedroom mini blinds with a vengeance. Tamra shielded her eyes and moaned with disbelief at how quickly morning had come. She rolled over to greet Joe Joe but he wasn't there. That was the best rest she had gotten in weeks…maybe months. It was amazing how safe and secure she felt around her husband. He was a shell of his former self now and she would still trust him with her life.

Joe Joe's transformation didn't happen overnight. In the aftermath of all that happened, he sprung into action. He made funeral arrangements, found somewhere for them to live, and even attempted to braid Jayla's hair. He took care of everything as if he had always been doing it. But as time passed, he began to talk less and drink more.

It started with a drink with dinner. Who could blame him? Then it was one when he got home and another with dinner. When Tamra had to add the local Wine & Spirits as a line item in the budget, she knew she had a major problem.

Tamra rolled out the bed and peered out the window just in time to see Joe Joepuling off to go to work. She turned the stereo on and Larry Colbert's CD began to blare from the speakers. She needed the inspiration.

"Jesus, you're the greatest," Tamra joined the call and response. She put the song on repeat, turned the volume up, took a deep breath and headed toward Jayla's room. She knew this would be a battle. Every Monday morning was. Tamra barged into her daughter's bedroom to find her kneeling at the side of her bed praying. *I'm having that dream again.* Tamra had a recurring dream that she was getting dressed and the morning was sailing by smoothly. She'd be on her way out the door when she realized it was a dream and she'd overslept. She was sure this was the case today.

She crept out of Jayla's room as to not interrupt her prayer and proceeded to get dressed for the day. With minimal effort, she got ready for work, grabbed her CD to listen to in the car and headed downstairs to the kitchen. Jayla was parked in front of the television dressed and half way through a bowl of Lucky Charms. Jayla had become more independent than a normal seven-year-old. She had gone from being the baby sister to an only child overnight. That made Tamra sad. She wished she could give her innocence back. Tamra filled her travel mug with coffee and they were ready to go.

"Our Father, which art in Heaven," Jayla's little voice came from the backseat. Tamra had started saying the Lord's Prayer every morning in the car. Soon, Jayla learned all the words and would begin it before Tamra got a chance to. Today was no different. They finished praying together and chatted until they pulled up in front of Jayla's bus stop. She hopped out of the car and ran toward the group of kids shoving for the first spot in line as the bus pulled up.

Tamra always felt a little uneasy seeing Jayla off to school. If anything ever happened to her, Tamra would undoubtedly lose it. She hated to think that way but she took the lives of her children for granted until she lost one. She wouldn't let that happen again.

Tamra kept an eye on Jayla's beads bopping down the aisle until she found her desired seat. She could see her turn around and talk to the little girl behind her. The bus driver looked into the rearview mirror and yelled at some boys goofing around. Without paying attention, the driver put the ten ton missile in drive and pulled into the intersection. She never saw a car blow right through the stop sign. The bus driver slammed on the brakes sending all the little passengers flying into the stiff, brown seats in front of them, avoiding collision. She redirected her verbal wrath at the young man driving the tinted boom box on wheels. Tamra screamed and jumped out the car to run to Jayla. But, the bus driver rolled her eyes at the careless driver, tooted the horn at Tamra and proceeded to barrel toward the next corner of waiting children.

Tamra got back in her car and took a big gulp of her coffee like it was a shot of alcohol. She breathed heavily trying to regain her composure. *You gotta calm down, Tam.* Her cell phone buzzed loudly in the center console of the car, rattling her nerves all over again. It was her sister.

They chatted briefly about what they did over the weekend and what the current week had in store. Her sister, Dennise, rushed off the phone after she accidentally called Jayla by Kya's name. Tamra and Dennise's relationship had changed in the last six months. But, Tamra couldn't think of one relationship in her life that hadn't. She didn't take it personally. People didn't know what to say to her and sometimes she just didn't feel like talking anyway.

Tamra got to work with seconds to spare and her phone was already ringing. After the first phone call, a million more of them followed. There was finally a break in the action just long enough for her to overhear her co-worker yapping loudly on the phone about her daughter's birthday party coming up.

"She better be lucky she's living to see another year," her co-worker said into the phone. "I almost killed her with that attitude she brought home from her dad's this weekend."

Tamra's heart sank and her eyes filled up. She should have been planning Kya's 10th birthday party next month. Instead, there would be awkward silence. She felt thunder in her stomach, lightning in her head, and the black cloud was rolling in. A Category 5 depression was brewing and a torrential downpour of tears was near. Her office phone rang again. Saved by an irate insurance agent.

***

The rest of Monday and all of Tuesday seemed to go by without any noteworthy events. Wednesday was the same. Tamra began to perk up the closer the clock got to 5:00. She knew she was that much closer to bible study. As a newcomer to the church and everything related to it, she looked forward to actually learning about Christianity. Sunday morning service reminded her why she should be saved. Wednesday night taught her how.

Tamra and Jayla were the first members to arrive at the church, just like most weeks. Jayla jumped out of the car and ran to Pastor Givens who was standing outside talking to a gentleman Tamra had never seen at the church before. Pastor and the man seemed well acquainted so she assumed he had been a member before she joined. Tamra grabbed her purse and church bag from the backseat of the car and walked toward the church doors.

Jayla was excitedly talking to them about her day when Tamra approached them. She hugged Pastor Givens, squeezing her eyes closed anticipating his three signature thumps on the back. After her windpipes had been involuntarily cleared, she turned and greeted the other man. She extended her hand to say hello and he pulled her into a hug. Yup, he must've been a member.

"God bless you, Sister."

His voice was raspy but extremely friendly. He smelled like CK One and his embrace was firm. Tamra smoothed her pencil skirt out, as he gave her the once over. She did the same to him. He looked to be about 6 feet tall and of average build. His eyes were light brown and mysterious. He seemed to look through Tamra, like they shared a secret. That made her uncomfortable. She focused on his mouth as he exchanged pleasantries with her. His lips were slightly darker than his hazelnut skin. Tamra suspected that he smoked. But, they were plump and looked soft. She resisted the urge to reach out and touch them. His eyes continued to bore into her. She readjusted her purse on her shoulder and began to finger the locket dangling from her necklace. She always did that when she was nervous. He started to say something and was interrupted.

Jayla tugged on Tamra's arm and asked if they could go inside. The contents of her church bag spilled out and Jayla's tambourine went clamoring down the steps like a slinky. Jayla raced down them after it, tripping and falling down each and every concrete step. She wailed like an infant and Tamra felt like she couldn't get to her fast enough. She scooped Jayla off the sidewalk and hurried inside to the ladies' room, leaving Pastor Givens and the man with the haunting eyes to gather the scattered papers that were fluttering in the autumn wind.

Tamra plopped Jayla on top of the counter in the bathroom, inspecting her from head to toe. She took her shredded stockings off and placed a wet paper towel on her bleeding knee. Her cries echoed and bounced off the stalls in the bathroom. Tamra just shook her head at the theatrics.

Jayla had always been dramatic. She acted as if every scrape was a gushing wound and every joke was Richard Pryor live. Always over the top. Tamra often called her Erica Kane...such an actress. And she was giving a stellar performance at that very moment. Tamra played along. She knew that her baby's pride was hurt more than her knee. She hugged her tightly, rocked her back and forth and began to hum the first melody she could make up. Jayla's cries decreased to a moan and ended in a whimper.

Tamra picked Jayla up off the counter and headed out the bathroom door. The man from outside was standing there waiting with her bag...still staring.

"You have a beautiful voice," he said. She stuttered a thank you, as he handed her the bag. He followed her upstairs and she blushed when she realized she was switching her hips. This man, whoever he was, was attractive but she was still married. And although she and Joe Joe lived more like college freshman roommates, they were married all the same. She loved him and deep down under all his pain and silence, she knew he loved her, too. By the time Tamra got to her seat, she felt guilty; although, she hadn't done anything. She physically shook her head in an attempt to shake her thoughts out of her head.

Bible study began and Pastor Givens was elated to give an announcement.

There's a new church joining the fold," the congregation hooped and hollered. "And our dear friend from Philadelphia, Pennsylvania will be the pastor!" They continued to cheer. "It is my pleasure to present to some and introduce to others, Elder Elijah McCall!" The church acted like Frankie Beverly and Maze had just been announced to give an A and B selection.

Tamra looked around and felt out of place for not cheering like a groupie. She didn't understand. Then, she heard him speak. Her eyes darted to the pulpit and none other than Ol' Brown Eyes was looking right back at her. *He's a preacher?* She wanted to crawl under the pew.

"God bless you, Saints. I bring you greetings from Faith and Holy Deliverance where the pastor is Bishop Edward McCall, Sr." More applause.

"It makes my heart glad to report to you today that God is still on the throne and He is yet working miracles." He waited for everyone to calm down just to rile them up again.

"I'm a Philly boy. But, God is sending me out like Joshua and Caleb. I declare that I will come back with a good report! I'll be heading a church in the great city of Reading. However, I'm going to spend some time with you all. Is that all right? I've come to Bible Tabernacle tonight in good ol' Harrisburg, P – A for a little help. Now ya'll know I'm a single man. Will you come check on me from time to time?" All the women gladly hollered that they would. "Make sure I have a good meal every now and again?" The women were willing to do that too. "And will you pray for me? Ask God to give me the words to say that SOULS will be saved." The church members screamed yes and waved in his direction.

Tamra still didn't feel comfortable acting like she was in the front row of a rap concert at church. She definitely felt moved at church. That's why she was there every time the doors opened. She just wasn't as moved as some of the others, apparently. She figured it would come with time.

"Our God in Heaven," Elder McCall began to pray. His voice dropped to just above a whisper. Everyone immediately lowered their heads. Tamra signaled to Jayla to sit still and she closed her eyes. It didn't take long for Elder McCall's voice to crescendo into a growl as he summoned God. She could hear that he was moving around. Without notice, she felt a huge hand slap her on the forehead. Her eyes shot open in surprise to find Elder McCall's palm gripping her entire head. She was shocked that she hadn't blacked out like everyone else did on Sundays when Pastor Givens laid hands on them. He handed the microphone to Minister Michaels who took over praying for the rest of the congregation. Elder McCall prayed specifically for Tamra.

He kept praying for peace. It seemed like it was the only word he was saying. She felt her hands begin to shake and she started to plead for peace along with him. He pulled her to the front of the church and fiery tears singed her cheek. Tamra wanted to turn and run out of the church like a track star. She knew what was coming next. This man was about to tell everyone all her business. Except something kept her feet planted at the altar. She tightly squeezed his hand. Unsure of what he was going to say, she knew she needed to hear it.

Minister Michaels brought the mic back to Elder McCall and waited a moment before he spoke, as if to gather his words and align them correctly.

"You are a zombie," his words were slow and drawn out. "You are walking. You're talking. You go to work, come to church, take care of your house and you're DEAD!" His voice jumped two octaves on the last word. "When my God is done with you, you will be as Lazarus. I...speak...life." He put his hand back on her forehead, the congregation went up in praise and Tamra felt like someone had turned all the lights off.

When she came to, the stirring sounds of the organ had been replaced with everyone singing a soft, melodic rendition of Amazing Grace. Some of the women helped her up and back to her seat. They gave her a handful of tissues and a small wax cup. As quickly as she gulped down the half of a swallow of lukewarm water, it seemed bible study was dismissed. Tamra had never even pulled her bible out her bag.

Chapter 3

That night, Tamra laid in the bed thinking. Elder McCall's words replayed in her head jabbing at her like a knife. The truth has a tendency to cut deep. She turned on her side, positioned her body pillow between her knees and prepared to fall asleep. Yet, she only kept thinking. Her mind wouldn't shut off. She squeezed her eyes shut and her thoughts began to play like a movie.

When it happened, Easter had just passed and the April air smelled like rain and new life. When the Jordan family went to bed that night, they had no clue everything would be different in the morning. Joe Joe and Tamra were knocked out after staying up late whispering and giggling like teenagers. They had wondered aloud if the girls heard them making love and eventually fell asleep in each other's arms. It was unlikely that Kya and Jayla heard a peep since their rooms were up on the third floor. But, Jayla was a light sleeper and would probably wake her big sister if she heard the slightest noise.

Joe Joe woke up first in the wee hours of that morning. He sputtered and coughed as he inhaled smoke in his sleep. Tamra was oblivious to the conditions of the air quality. She had pulled the covers over her head hours before to escape the tundra Joe Joe had to sleep in. He gasped and yelled Tamra's name to wake her but the smoke rushed in his mouth forcing his words back down. He shook her violently pushing her onto the floor. She jolted awake and panic covered her like a duvet. She frantically felt around for any article of clothing. Hardly anything was visible in the room and the black, billowing smoke made it unbearable for her to keep her eyes open. Tamra and Joe Joe made it to the bedroom door almost at the same time. He pushed her toward the steps to go downstairs. He began to crawl up the stairs to the girls' rooms. When Tamra got to the bottom of the steps, she heard Jayla crying in fear. She barely made out the outline of her daughters in the dining room.

"They're down here!" Tamra yelled up to Joe Joe. She almost vomited from soot and fear. It seemed to take Joe Joe forever to get to the first floor. He ushered them out of the house. Tamra rubbed her eyes and took long deep breaths of the damp, spring air. The faint sound of fire engine sirens seemed a world away. Neighbors were filing out of their houses. A few of them were screaming on the phone for the fire department to hurry. At this rate, the entire row of homes would burn to the ground. Someone approached them with blankets to cover Tamra and the kids when the windows of the house connected to theirs burst, sending shards of glass flying in every direction. Everyone ran for cover. The nice lady from a few doors down who had kids that played with the girls hurried over to make sure they were okay.

"Oh, my Lord!" she shrieked. "Are you alright? Where's your daughter?"

Tamra looked down and located Jayla who was trembling with trepidation. She looked at Joe Joe, who was a few feet away, but he didn't have Kya. Her eyes scanned the crowd, which was increasing by the second. But, none of them were Kya. Tamra ran over to Joe Joe, pulling Jayla in tow. She was running as fast as her feet would move but she felt like she was wading through quicksand.

Tamra yelled Kya's name at the top of her lungs. Everyone immediately began to look around in search of her.

"Where is she," Tamra said out loud. She turned to Jayla. "Jay Jay, where's Sissie?" Jayla stared blankly. Tamra shook her. "Where's Sissie, Jay Jay?" Tamra screamed.

"She wouldn't wake up," Jayla said softly. At that moment, Tamra realized that the second outline she saw standing in the dining room was Jayla's "Just My Size" life-size doll that was now stiffly standing next to her staring just as blankly as her daughter.

Tamra turned to bolt toward the house. Joe Joe must have read her mind. He grabbed her around the waist and barked for the first responders who had finally arrived to rescue her. They acted immediately. But, immediately wasn't fast enough for Tamra. She twisted her body, freeing herself of her husband's grasp and only left him holding the blanket she had been wrapped in. She pushed through the gate, tearing the night shirt she had managed to grab on her way out and bound up the stairs two at a time. She ignored Joe Joe calling her and Jayla crying "Mommy". She took one long drag of fresh air and raced into the house.

The heat was sweltering. She felt like she had run a marathon within the first five seconds of entering the house. She wanted to call out for Kya but her chest tightened each time she opened her mouth. She leaned against the wall to feel her way to the staircase and it felt like she had lain directly on an open flame. After what felt like hours, she got near the top of the steps and saw the entire second floor engulfed in flames. The wooden banister that had protected the girls from falling, when they were little, crackled from the heat of the flames. It sounded as if it was holding on to its security with all its might. She grabbed it to hoist herself onto the last step and heard it creak and then snap loudly. The banister gave way and it and Tamra went crashing down the steps. Exhausted, burned, and pinned under what was left of the solid oak railing, Tamra turned her head and looked to the very spot she thought she had last seen Kya. She closed her eyes hoping she would awake from this nightmare to find her soundly sleeping in her bed.

Tamra sat straight up in her bed. She gasped for air to prove that she was dreaming and she wasn't actually back in the fire again. Tears sprang from her eyes as guilt lay in the bed with her where her husband used to be. She knew he blamed her. He was on his way to save them when she told him they were both downstairs. She thought she saw them. How could she not know her own daughter from a doll? And then she thought of those precious moments that were wasted before she even realized Kya was still in the house. Her baby was being burned alive while she stood wondering how she would be able to re-buy a house full of belongings. Part of Tamra hoped she'd be able to battle the flames and drag Kya to safety. Another part of her wanted to die at the bottom of those steps the same way Kya had, for making such a horrible mistake.

Tamra scooted over and let regret wrap its arms around her and hold her tight. It stroked her hair and rubbed her back and reminded her of all the things she should have done differently that night. She allowed it. She deserved each and every terrible thought she had about herself. Her daughter had died on that fateful night six months ago. She couldn't help but to think it was her fault.

Realistically, Tamra could have done nothing to save Kya that night. It started due to faulty electrical wiring next door. The fire marshal told them that it started on the second floor and spread so quickly that she was trapped before she even knew she needed to get out. They later found her barricaded in the corner. She pulled the mattress on top of her to shield her from the flames. She likely lost consciousness as the fire inched toward her, ravaging the items in her room that she so dearly loved. They said she didn't suffer. Tamra was doing enough for the both of them, now.

The funeral services were a blur. Tamra walked down the aisle of the church with Joe Joe practically holding her up. Her eyes were full of tears and the casket seemed incredibly short. Just like Kya's life. No chance to grow to what it should have been. Flowers were everywhere. They surrounded the pearl pink box she laid in. Tamra felt nauseous as they approached it.

"You don't have to do this," Joe Joe whispered.

She ignored his concern, took a deep breath and peered at her baby. Her lungs deflated and air escaped her mouth. She fought the urge to climb in with her. Instead, she ran her fingers through her curls. Tamra could never get her hair to look like that. She noticed a hint of colored lip gloss. Kya would have been elated.

"I'm right here," Joe Joe said. Tamra nodded her head and one big tear fell from her eyelashes onto the satin sleeve of her angel. Tamra touched everything in the casket, in an attempt to fix it. She ran her fingers over the little Bible, straightened the teddy bear Kya was clutching, and adjusted and readjusted the same strand of hair a million times. She was always able to fix everything. However, Tamra couldn't bring herself to touch Kya's skin.

The funeral directors called for the final viewing and they tried to usher Tamra to her seat while everyone filed by the coffin for the last time. She refused to move. She stood near Kya's head…fixing her curl. People tried to hug Tamra and give words of encouragement but she hardly realized they were there. She still couldn't believe she was actually there. Every time someone kissed Kya, Tamra would fix everything in the casket all over again.

The seemingly endless line slowed up and Joe Joe brought Jayla up to view her big sister for the last time. Then it was Tamra's turn. Kya's cheeks looked so plump. The corners of her mouth turned up as if she was smiling. Her skin was bronze and seemed to radiate. Tamra braced herself to lean in closer. The lining of the casket felt as soft as a cloud. Tamra kissed her daughter's cheek and she was ice cold. It sent a chill through her entire body. She regretted her choice for one last kiss. She should have stuck to fixing her curls.

She finally sat in her seat and the funeral directors turned the two floor lamps off that anchored the coffin. They then stood next to each other and slowly lowered the lid to the box. It seemed to take forever. Tamra lowered her eyes with the lid to try to catch every glimpse of Kya as possible. They shut the casket, sealed it shut, and placed a huge bouquet of white lilies on top. They methodically turned and began a processional down the aisle. Tamra dropped her head and cried throughout the entire service.

Tamra felt around in the bed for the remote, turned the television on, and turned the volume up. She clicked to the T.V. Guide channel and pretended to look for something to watch. It was 5:17 a.m. She just needed something to drown out the thoughts in her head. Once she started thinking about Kya's death, she couldn't force herself to stop. It had to play all the way out. Tamra was just waiting for her real life nightmare to go off.

The bedroom door cracked open and the hallway light illuminated the room. Tamra's eyes adjusted to find Jayla creeping into the room. She shut the door harder than they both expected and scurried across the carpet and hopped in the bed with Tamra. Tamra was happy to see her. She'd much rather have Jayla snuggling with her than her own guilt. She grabbed a loose strand of her baby's hair and twirled it between her fingers until she drifted back to sleep. Sweet dreams and rest came to her just minutes before her alarm went off.

Chapter 4

Tamra got to work and was greeted with an Outlook reminder that she had a therapy session later that afternoon. It couldn't have come on a better day. Coffee and prayer got her through the morning. Routine and the grace of God got her out to Progress Avenue for her appointment.

Tamra got settled in the chair at Dr. Steele's office and tugged at her necklace. Dr. Steele didn't speak until she lowered her hand.

"You ready?" A warm and inviting smile spread across Dr. Steele's face. She was beautiful in an exotic kind of way. She had flawless, dark skin with pronounced cheek bones. Her hair was thick and coarse. The deep waves in it indicated it was natural. She was thin as a rail and when she crossed her long legs her foot still almost touched the floor.

Tamra took a deep breath and began. She started with the dream and talked until her mouth got dry. Dr. Steele took an occasional note here and there but, for the most part, she listened to Tamra talk. Tamra felt comfortable with Dr. Steele from the first time they had met. She was open and direct with Tamra. Tamra recalled their first session just weeks after the fire. Dr. Steele got straight to Tamra's preconceived notions.

"I'm pretty sure you're uneasy about being here. A lot of our people don't seek therapy. You may think I'm just here to listen to you tell all your business. And the only thing that has stopped you from running out that door is the fact that I'm a 'sista.'" She used air quotes.

"I know that this is abnormal for you, Mrs. Jordan. On the other hand, what in your life is normal, right now? Additionally, I'm more than another Black woman. I take my job very seriously. No matter what the reason is that brought you into my office, I am hoping you give me a chance to work with you until we get your life back to normal."

Either Tamra had accidentally doubled up on her antidepressants that day or this woman was actually a good fit. Whatever the case was, Tamra thought it was worth a shot and she was now glad she had kept coming back. Against the counsel of everyone in her life, Tamra stuck with therapy and felt much stronger because of it.

"So when do you plan on moving forward with your life, Tamra?" She asked matter-of-factly.

"Excuse me?" Tamra was caught off guard.

"When do you plan on moving forward with your life?" She repeated the question as if it had made sense the first time.

"I'm not suggesting that you forget about what happened or what you had before it happened. Still, I want to have honest dialogue about where you go now that it has. You've still got a lot of life ahead of you. I want you to start thinking about what you want out of that life. What makes YOU happy?"

She sat back in her plush office chair and shut her leather padfolio. "I will be out of town next week so I'll see you the week after, okay?"

Hopefully, you're getting some therapy of your own, Tamra thought to herself. How could Dr. Steele drop a question like that for her to ponder and then smile like nothing happened? Tamra was thankful for excellent healthcare benefits. She was certain she'd be needing therapy for a very long time to come!

By the time Tamra got home that evening, she was exhausted. Her mom called and asked if Jayla could spend the night and go to school from her house. Normally, Tamra was a stickler about no sleepovers on school nights, but she was too tired to argue. She packed Jayla's things and waved from the front door as her mom's car pulled away.

She went right upstairs and lay across the bed. The silence of the house was calming. It was rare that the house was so quiet. But, Tamra liked the noise. She slipped out of her work clothes and grabbed a tank top from the top drawer.

Her hand grazed against the silicone she kept buried beneath her undergarments. She looked over her shoulder to make sure no one was there. For some reason, her toys always made her nervous. Like she was doing something she shouldn't. She pushed the bedroom door closed, switched the batteries around and laid back across her bed. She instinctively turned the volume of the television up just a bit and let her eyes roll back.

She let the humming noise drown out the TV and the stress of her day. She imagined it was Joe Joe. She missed him; the way he touched her and felt inside her. She longed for the days that they talked. In moments like this, she yearned for the way he made her body feel. Just as she was about to release, she got mad. *This is ridiculous!* Her husband was down two flights of stairs and she was imagining.

Tamra got right up and pranced down the steps. She trotted down the basement steps and stood behind Joe Joe's recliner, resting her forearms behind his head.

"Hey, Tam."

"Hey, Joey Baby." He turned around and looked at her. She knew she had caught him off guard. She sat on the arm of the chair. He noticed she had nothing on but a tank top and a thong. His eyebrows shot up and he looked toward the step.

"She's at my mom's for the night," Tamra said answering his unspoken question as to Jayla's whereabouts. She slid off the chair and into his lap. She propped her feet where she had just been sitting. He ran his hand down the outside of her leg then began to run it up the inside.

"I miss you, Joey." He squeezed the inside of her thigh then ran his finger along the outside of her underwear. He pushed them aside and plunged his finger deep inside her. She drenched his hand.

"You do miss me, huh?" He growled. She could feel him harden beneath her. She kissed him forcibly and positioned her body to straddle him. Her lips never left his. An involuntary moan came from deep within her. She didn't even want to think about how long it had been. Tamra fumbled with his belt and unbuttoned his pants.

"No." She heard him say it but didn't want to believe it. Just before total disappointment set in, he took her hand and led her to their bedroom. He rummaged through the drawers of the nightstand to find a lighter to light a candle. He seemed like a visitor in the house he owned.

Tamra watched as the flame cast his shadow across the wall. His presence seemed to fill the room. He let his work pants drop to the floor and he stood over her just looking at her, biting his bottom lip. He began to kiss her all over. His lips felt new and familiar at the same time. His tongue stopped between her thighs and he professed his love for what seemed like an eternity. By the time he entered her, she thought she would faint from ecstasy.

Once again, his presence filled the area it was in. Tamra whimpered and it turned Joe Joe on. She felt like he was looking for something. With each thrust, he seemed to be trying to close the gap between them. Their bodies communicated in a way their voices had been unable to before. They climaxed and Tamra never felt closer to her husband.

Joe Joe stood up and swooned a bit. She wrapped her legs around his waist and pulled him back down on top of her. She ran her fingertips up and down the center of his back. He shuttered and she giggled. Tamra planted kisses on the top of his head and prayed that the pieces to their puzzle were about to start snapping back into place.

Joe Joe gave her a deep, passionate kiss and pulled his pants up from around his ankles.

"I need a drink," he stated and headed for the door. So much for that.

Tamra woke up the next morning a little off kilter. She got to sleep in since Jayla wasn't home. She needed the extra sleep. She had stayed up late thinking about her relationship with Joe Joe...if you could even call it that. She couldn't keep living like this. But, she worried that Jayla would be heartbroken if Joe Joe left. Though, for all Tamra knew, Joe Joe was already gone.

Chapter 5

Dennise had called while Tamra was getting dressed and asked for a ride downtown. Her car was acting up again. Tamra pulled up in front of her sister's house and beeped for her to come out. Tamra saw her lean in the door and kiss someone then burst into laughter like a schoolgirl. She was still chuckling when she got in the car.

"Don't ask because it's none of your business," were the first words out of her mouth.

"I'll ask any question I want to ask in MY car," Tamra snapped. "And what makes you think I give a damn who you're loving now?" They both sat in silence for a second. Then Tamra spoke again.

"Is that Eric?"

"Yes, Girl! He is back and in full effect!" They both started laughing.

Dennise and Eric had the classic love-hate relationship. They broke up and got back together more times than Tamra could count. She wished her sister would leave Eric once and for all but apparently Dennise enjoyed the crap he put her through. She was Eric's safe haven. He always called her when he needed some type of help. She'd get him out of one jam or another then he'd disappear for awhile. Tamra didn't understand it, but maybe to her little sister, a little bit of him was better than none at all.

"Well, I guess we both have that morning after glow," Tamra joked.

"Who'd you get some from?" Dennise exclaimed.

"My husband!"

"Oh," she seemed disappointed.

"Why did you say it like that?"

Dennise looked like she was going to let it go at first then decided against that idea.

"I'm just sayin...you know I love you...and Joe Joe's cool and all..." Dennise seemed to be choosing her words wisely so she wouldn't hurt Tamra's feelings.

"Look, he needs to decide what he's going to do. Either he's going to be with you or not. How I see it, you're the side jawn and his bottle is his main chick. Point, blank, period." She gazed out the passenger side window satisfied she had gotten that off her chest.

"You have some nerve, Dennise! You're bumming rides off me to go to work while you let that no good Negro lay up in your house. He probably won't even be there when you get home. And furthermore, I am married. Try staying off your back long enough to prove that you're marriage material."

"Is that what Bishop Slick Talk is teaching ya'll down at Bible Tabernacle? Where can I sign up to be a Christian like you, Tam?" Dennise asked in the most sarcastic tone she could muster.

They rode in silence again. No jokes to serve as an apology. Just hurt feelings and a traffic jam to prolong their misery.

Tamra knew that her sister didn't hate Joe Joe. She loved him like a brother. But, her loyalty was to Tamra. And Dennise made no secrets about how she felt about her big sister. If Tamra loved you, Dennise loved you, too. But, all it took was for someone to look at Tamra sideways once and Dennise was ready to throw down. Tamra appreciated how much she loved her. But she also knew she had to be careful what she told her. Dennise had a big mouth and a long memory.

Tamra had barely tapped the brake in front of Dennise's job before her sister was half way out the car. She muttered a thank you and huffed to the door. Tamra just had to shake her head and laugh. Dennise had probably already forgotten why she was mad but would keep the attitude anyway.

When Tamra got to her desk, there was a Post-It note stuck to her computer screen with a message for her to go see her supervisor. She didn't have to read the note to know who it was from. The white paper with the gerbera daisy border and fluorescent ink bright enough to cause an instant migraine was a dead giveaway. Tamra swore there was a 13 year-old girl trapped inside her boss's body dying to come out and attend a Jonas Brothers concert. She put her purse in her desk drawer, picked up a pen and tablet, and headed toward the office.

"You wanted to see me, Megan."

"Heyyy, Tamraaah." She always drug out the last syllable of the word she was saying. She put away the colored lip gloss she was applying that made the office smell like strawberry frosting.

"As you know, annual reviews are coming up. Not that you would have anything to worry about anyway but we're just going to waive yours this year. You'll get the standard raise."

Tamra wanted to tell her that what she just said made no sense but since Tam had been dealing with her for so long, she knew what she meant. Honestly, what she really wanted to tell her was that she's an idiot and she should stop dying her hair with Kool-Aid packets. But, she figured that wouldn't end well.

Tam said okay, spun on her heels, and headed back to her desk. The first thing she did was prepare a folder of information for an annual review. She had suffered great loss in the past year. Her brain wasn't among the items gone. They would never have a reason to question Tamra's ability to do her job.

Her position as a case manager at a life insurance brokerage firm wasn't hard. It was just a lot. She had the highest case load on the team and the most difficult insurance agents would only deal with her. The worst thing Tamra could have ever done after accepting her position some years ago was prove herself to be competent. Now they expected her to work miracles on a daily basis. Her touch of OCD made her continue to try to perform them.

Tamra's work phone rang and she saw her dad's number pop up on the caller ID.

"Hey, Dad!" Her spirits were instantly lifted.

"Baby Girl, what have I told you and your sister about arguing?"

"Oh, Daddy. It's nothing. How are you?"

He coughed loudly into the phone.

"You still haven't been to the doctor," she scolded.

"I'll go when I'm good and ready. I'm the parent here," he reminded her. "Besides, I don't have time to go to the doctor when my girls are always going at it like two men in a bar brawl."

Tamra just laughed. She should have known Dennise would call and "tell" on her. She'd told her sister a million times to stop doing that. Their dad worried just to have something to worry about. And when it came to them, it didn't take much to get him all worked up.

For as long as she could remember, their dad bent over backward to protect Tamra, Dennise, and their older brother Shawn. Their real mother had gotten sick one day when they were very young, went to the hospital, and never came back. Tamra later found out she was in a mental ward for two years. She went to live with her sister and committed suicide less than 24 hours after being there. Most people in the family pretended she never existed and prayed that the crazy gene wasn't hereditary.

"Daddy, I'll call Dennise and apologize." That was the only way he'd let her off the phone. Tamra immediately called her sister and cussed her out between clinched teeth. Her dad called her back five minutes later.

"I'm gon' kill that girl," Tamra said aloud.

Once Tam started thinking about her sister, she started thinking about what Dennise had said in the car. Joe Joe was treating her like a mistress. He gave Tamra a little time here and there and always left her feeling like he'd come back. But, ultimately, he always left her and went back to the basement. She kept telling herself that he was sick. Leaving him now would send him deeper into depression. It would eventually kill him. But, Tam knew she was risking her own life if she stayed.

Chapter 6

Tamra woke up Sunday morning with a renewed mind and a rested body. She got to church even earlier than normal to make sure the church was in order from the wedding that was held the day before. She sang to herself as she vacuumed the sanctuary. The plush red carpet changed shades as she pushed the stick vac back and forth over it. It reminded her of how she often heard people in church refer to Jesus's blood cleansing their sins. She sure hoped they were right.

The more Tamra came to church, the more she wondered if getting into Heaven was possible. She had the basics down before she attended Bible Tabernacle. She didn't make a habit of lying. She didn't cheat or steal. She knew a few of the Ten Commandments and did pretty well with those. But, Pastor Givens gave so many instructions on how to be a Christian. Between Sunday service, bible study, and this newcomer's class she'd be starting, Tamra was sure she'd be failing the final exam at the pearly gates.

Sort of like a person wearing headphones, the vacuum drowned out the volume of her voice, making her unaware of how loud she was singing to begin with. She belted out the lyrics to "I Know I've Been Changed." Tamra was no LaShun Pace but, she was sure singing like she was. Just as she got to the good part, Tamra looked up and saw Elder McCall standing there smiling.

"You betta sang!" He teased her and began to laugh. Tamra prayed that God would open the sky and take her up in the rapture right then and there. She wanted to keel over from embarrassment.

She quickly cut the sweeper off and followed the chord to the plug in the wall. She sat on the end of the front pew and began to wrap the chord up. She wanted to turn around to see if he had walked out of the room. But, the increasingly present scent of his cologne indicated he was still there. And he was coming toward her. The bench was about 10 feet long but he decided to sit next to her with less than an inch between them.

"Tamra, right?"

"Yes."

"Why don't you like me?"

"I beg your pardon?" Tamra was confused.

"You heard me, Girl! What'd I do to you? I chased your church notes down the street for you after you pushed your little girl down the steps and I complimented your singing twice. You still have no words for me. What's up with that?"   Tamra sat in total shock and didn't know how to respond. He spoke before she could.

"Oh, I get it. I'm a minister so you expect me to be all stiff and proper. Let us pray."

He dropped his head and started an overly dramatic prayer. Tamra giggled.

"My Lord! Prayer changes things," he exclaimed.

Tamra fell out laughing. She felt a little embarrassed for overlooking Elder McCall as a human just because he was a preacher. He could preach and pray. But, he was funny, too. And he had a genuine smile. And he was sexy. Tamra caught herself staring at his lips like she had the other day outside the church.

"So tell me about yourself." He put his arm on the back of the pew behind her.

"What would you like to know?" She wondered if he heard the involuntary flirtation in her voice.

"Let's start with your full name." If he had heard it, he ignored it. She was a tad disappointed.

"Tamra Baker-Jordan."

"Well, it's a pleasure to finally have a name to match that beautiful voice of yours. He patted her on the back. They were about to continue talking.

Suddenly, someone coughed behind them with the clear intent to make their presence know. Tamra shot up out of the seat and turned to see who it was. Elder McCall never flinched, though. Tamra's stomach dropped. It was Tawonda Miller. She could sing like an angel but gossiped like the devil. Tamra hurriedly finished wrapping the vacuum chord up.

"So sorry to interrupt, Elder," Tawonda shot Tamra a look. "But, is there anything I can do for you before service starts?"

Tamra heard him politely tell her no as she walked away.

"Ms. Baker-Jordan," he called after her. Both Tamra and Tawonda looked at him intensely.

"You keep singing, ya hear?" He flashed a bright smile at her and turned his attention back to Tawonda.

Tamra ran down the steps and went into the bathroom. She put her hand on her forehead and tried to slow the racing thoughts in her mind. She hoped that it didn't appear to Tawonda that Tamra was hitting on Elder McCall. But, from what little she knew of the scandal loving soprano, it didn't matter at this point. The story was as good as told. If Tamra wanted to be honest with herself, for a change, she was flirting with that man. She *would* have been if Tawonda hadn't cleared her windpipe at that very moment.

Tamra heard the sound again. It startled her for a second time. She opened her eyes and saw Tawonda's reflection in the mirror behind her. Tamra had never heard her come in.

"Do you need a cough drop, Honey?" Tamra didn't have one to offer. But, it was clear Tawonda caught on to her sarcasm and had a little of her own.

"Hey, Tanya. Where's Jada?" Her eyebrow shot up and she smirked as she emphasized each name.

"That's Tamra and Jayla isn't here." Tam emphasized the names, too.

Tawonda leaned against the bathroom doorway.

"You know, it's been a while since I went through newcomer's class; but I'm pretty sure you shouldn't be tryna knock off a minister with a husband at home."

And, I've never taken singing lessons," Tamra countered. "But all that yelling you do is unnecessary."

The whole encounter felt like being in the high school gym locker room. Tamra wanted to get out of it fast. She was trying hard not to cuss this girl out, but she was testing Tam. The side that Bible Tabernacle never got to see of Tamra was the one that would leave Tawonda on the bathroom floor searching for her teeth. Tamra pushed passed her and waited for her to respond. She didn't. *She don't want none.*

Service started and Tamra tried to focus. She had gone from staring into Elijah McCall's eyes to about to punch Tawonda Miller in hers in a matter of seconds. Both incidents loomed over her. They made her think of hypocrisy in the church. She struggled with relating to preachers. Before joining church, she always viewed them as being closer to God than an average person. When she started attending Bible Tabernacle, she saw there was an entire congregation that thought the same way. But, as Elder McCall pointed out, they are human too. As for Tawonda, Tamra thought that saints like her were laughable. They were more two-faced than Siamese twins. They sat in church and pretended to be holier than thou and went home and raised Hell. Tawonda didn't even wait to get home!

As if on cue, the organ revved up and Tawonda started shouting. Her borderline stripper heels pounded into the carpet right where she stood earlier eavesdropping. She sounded like a jackhammer hard at work. Tamra rolled her eyes as crocodile tears seeped from Tawonda's. Tam couldn't shake her attitude so she just folded her arms and waited for church to be over.

Once everyone settled down, Pastor Givens notified everyone that it was time for the Word. Elder McCall stood in the pulpit and began to preach. Tamra didn't hear much of what he was saying though. Instead, she allowed her mind to drift. She thought about Elijah McCall, the man. What he must be like outside the church and why he was single. There was certainly no shortage of unmarried women around willing to fight each other gladiator style to snag a man. And Elijah McCall was the kind of man that made women feel like they were the only ones in the room when he spoke to them. Just the few short conversations they had made Tamra think about joining the fight for him.

She snapped out of her thoughts and hoped no one had seen her licking her lips. She listened to what he was talking about. It was as if he had been reading her mind.

"We call ourselves Christian, but don't act like Christ. Sittin' in church preaching to each other. In the bible, Jesus was rarely in the church. He was out among the people…making the blind to see and the lame to walk. And ya'llscared to serve a bowl of soup at the Bethesda Mission but wanna bring the pastor some orange juice in a goblet. Amen, somebody?" The congregation agreed.

After service was over, all those that had joined church within the last month had a meeting. Pastor Givens explained to them that Elder McCall would be teaching the newcomer's classes for eight weeks. Tamra was happy about that. He gave a synopsis of the information that would be given and the expectations of the five people that would be attending. Tamra really wasn't concerned about that. She just saw this as another opportunity to see Elder McCall. As soon as that thought crossed her mind, another chance presented itself. Pastor Givens dismissed the meeting and pulled Tamra aside.

"I need a huge favor, Sister Jordan."

"Sure, Pastor."

"I need to go down to the Bethesda Mission this afternoon. Elder McCall is staying at the Hampton Inn on Union Deposit. That's near you, right?

"Right around the corner."

"Would you be so kind to drop him off for me?"

"No problem, Pastor." Tamra's insides jumped.

Tamra threw a pair of shoes and an empty water bottle in the back seat before Elder McCall got in the car. He didn't waste any time getting the conversation started.

"It's just me and you, Tamra. Finish telling me about yourself."

"You should tell me something about you, Elder McCall. You haven't told me anything yet," she deflected the attention.

"First of all, it's Elijah. That title stuff is for people who are caught up on that type of thing. Second of all, I'm a Gemini and I like long walks on the beach." They both laughed.

"But, for real," he got very serious. "There's something about you, Tamra. I don't know what it is. And God hasn't told me anything bad about you. You know that's my homie. He gives me all the inside scoop."

"I'm married," she blurted out.

"My homie didn't tell me that." He sounded like an insulted child.

Tamra didn't know why she chose to divulge that information at that particular moment. Maybe she needed an excuse to stop herself from being turned on by him. Maybe she didn't trust herself to immediately leave that hotel parking lot after dropping him off. Or maybe she wanted him to be fully aware of what he would be soon repenting for.

"That's what it is, then." He said as if he had come to the revelation he was looking for. "We're both looking for something. Let's see if we can find it in each other."

He lightly swiped her hand as it rested on the gear of her car. Every nerve ending in her body stood at attention. He got out of the car and disappeared behind the automatic sliding glass doors of the hotel. Tamra sat and looked at the reflection of a woman who was going to cheat on her husband with a minister.

Chapter 7

By the time Tamra picked up Jayla and made it home, she had changed her mind a million times. At every stop sign, red light and turn, her decision seemed to change. She rationalized why it wasn't "technically" cheating. Then she replayed happy memories to make her fall back in love with Joe Joe.

When she pulled into the driveway, she was on Joe Joe. So she decided to stick with that decision. She fed Jayla, ironed clothes for the next day and tucked her into bed. Once back in her bedroom, she stood in front of the mirror and took a deep, cleansing breath. *You can do this.* Before her nerves got the best of her, she headed for the basement. She replayed Dennise's words from earlier in the week about her being a mistress to amp herself up. Tamra was ready for the fight of her life.

"Joe Joe?" Tamra nervously called down the steps. He lowered the volume of the TV and yelled to her that he was down there. She slowly walked down the stairs and asked him if they could talk. He cut the television off, set the remote down and picked up his glass. Tamra's eyes darted around the room. She was in search of all that confidence she had a minute ago. Joe Joe raised his eyebrows indicating that she could start talking at any moment.

"Joe Joe, you know I love you." She felt like she was on the set of Jerry Springer starting her speech out like that. "But, I need you to get some help. You're an alcoholic. I'll do whatever it takes to get you better. But, I'm losing you. Joey Baby, I love you."

Her words came out like the ammunition of an assault weapon. Each word flew out rapidly after the one before it with an intended target; his heart. Tamra felt tears forming. She looked at the ceiling to prevent them from spilling down her face. When her eyes returned to Joe Joe, it was as if he hadn't heard a word she said. He wasn't even paying her a cent's worth of attention. That pissed Tamra off.

"Did you hear what I said?"

She sounded like she was reprimanding Jayla, not professing her love and concern for her husband. He still didn't respond. Tamra stood in front of him and bent over to look him square in the eyes. He took another long sip from the glass. His attention was fully on his drink. He rested his hand on the arm rest of the chair and stared at the blank TV. It was as if she was invisible.

In an effort to make her presence and fury known, Tamra backhanded the half full glass out of Joe Joe's grasp. Hennessy went flying everywhere. She put her hands on her hips and mentally prepared a different approach. That confidence had come back.

"Joe Joe, I love you." This time she spoke with force. He lifted the bottom of his t-shirt and wiped his dripping face. She continued.

"I'm not gon' sit here and let you kill yourself. Get help or get out!"

He chuckled.

"You think this shit is funny?"

Joe Joe didn't verbally respond to her inquiry. Instead, he lunged from the chair and grabbed Tamra, pinning her arms at her sides. His fingers felt like vice grips. He shook her violently before throwing her to the floor. She cowered in fear as he kicked her in her back. The pain ripped through her. He knelt down on the carpet next to her with one knee holding her in place. He delivered blow after blow to her torso. Tamra screamed and pleaded for him to stop. She caught a glimpse of his face and she was looking into the eyes of the devil.

She tried to get away but his massive leg made her efforts futile. She was in the perfect position to take his flurry of punches and do nothing about them. She just loudly sobbed until they stopped. Joe Joe grabbed his bottle of liquor and emptied the contents all over Tamra's limp body. He sat back down, clicked the TV on, and proceeded to watch it. Tamra scurried upstairs, clawing at the steps. The muscles in her arms burned like fire. But, she knew she had to run to escape true Hell.

Tamra didn't stop running until she got to her bedroom and slammed and locked the door behind her. She slid down the door like the tears on her face. She pulled her knees into her chest. She opened her mouth and let out a sound and her own voice was foreign to her. It was more than a cry. It was the utterances of a broken soul.

Tam woke up the next day stiff, sore, and still curled up in a ball in front of the door. She limped to the master bathroom and winced when the steaming, hot water of the shower hit the red patches of her skin that were turning to bruises. She allowed the water to pelt those areas. Maybe the pain would help her brain to process that it actually had happened. Joe Joe had never put his hands on Tamra before. He used to find it hard to slap her ass during sex! So as much as it physically hurt, the shock of it was worse. She could not believe it.

Jayla knew something was wrong with Tam the second she finally stepped out of the bedroom that morning. Tam didn't have the strength to even try to hide it from her. Her face crinkled with pain. Her eyes looked past Jayla and searched for answers. There were none.

Tamra dropped Jayla off at school a few minutes late and didn't bother to go inside to sign her in. She just pulled off and cried the whole way to work. She quickly slipped past the conference room to avoid being seen by the team of supervisors in their Monday morning meeting. Once settled at her desk, she adjusted her throbbing body and began to throw herself full force into work. She fired off emails, made proactive phone calls, and ran reports to project her application to policy ratio for the rest of the year. Anything to take her mind off of last night.

Megan paged Tamra's phone and asked her to meet her in the conference room. She rolled her eyes, grabbed the folder in her top drawer and marched to the room. Just as she suspected, the supervisory team was seated around the table. Tamra grabbed an empty chair and sat down slowly. She clinched her jaw so they wouldn't see her pain.

"Tamra, as you know, it is the time of year that we conduct annual reviews."

Tamra couldn't help but laugh a little at Megan. Just days ago, she told her she wouldn't be getting one. Megan went through her little spiel and it was obvious she thought she was going to catch Tamra off guard. When would she learn?

"Well, Megan, even though you said I wouldn't be subjected to a review due to recent tragedies in my personal life, I took the liberty of preparing for one."

Tamra pulled out copies of the materials she prepared and passed them out.

"You'll notice that I've included a blank page for you to take notes on any comments, questions, or concerns you all may have for me."

Tamra proceeded to talk for ten minutes. She showed them bar graphs, statistical reports, and specific email print outs. When she was done, the team of five supervisors knew what goals she had surpassed, which ones she had yet to meet, how she would meet them and that she could do their job better than them on her worst day. She felt a headache coming on but wouldn't let her mind acknowledge it until she walked out of that conference room. After leaving them in awe of what she had just pulled off, she went to the vending machine. She needed the biggest gulp of caffeine she could get in her mouth.

She inserted the coins into the machine and pressed the button to dispense a Coke. Nothing happened. She pressed it a few more times and noticed she had been a nickel short.

"Awesome," she said sarcastically.

Tamra walked back to her desk and noticed someone sitting in her chair. She resisted the urge to choke the man from behind. She was just having that kind of day.

"Can I help you?"

Her attitude was on full blast. Her co-worker in the cubicle in front of her stopped what she was doing to see what was going on. The man in Tamra's chair spun around and she almost hit the floor.

"Quint! What are you doing here?" She couldn't believe it.

Quinton Davis. No words did a man like him justice. He and Tamra had been victims of bad timing. And as if he had an alarm clock set for "worst day ever to pop up," there he was in front of her.

"Tamra Baker. My girl!"

He jumped up out of the chair and pulled her into the biggest, tightest, most excruciating hug she had ever gotten. The tenderness of her beaten muscles were soon forgotten when she inhaled his scent. She immediately identified it as Fahrenheit. It tickled her nose, went to her head and immediately had an effect between her legs. This man…

When he finally let go of her, he stepped back and looked her up and down.

"You're looking good, Girl!" *Liar.*

"You ain't half bad, yourself," she replied.

Compared to Quint, Shemar Moore looked like Steve Urkel. He had that tall, dark, handsome, slow motion walk with a wind machine in the movies type of look. Gorgeous enough to make women sigh when he walked by. He always knew he looked good but he made everyone think that when they told him, it was the first time he had ever heard it.

"Come to lunch with me."

Tamra didn't bother to ask where or to let anyone in the office know she was leaving. She was sure all the nosey people within listening distance already knew. She grabbed her purse and they headed for the door. When they got outside, he ushered her to the shining, black Cadillac SRX he was driving. He opened the door and helped her in before joyfully running around to the driver side. He started the truck and the engine purred.

"Where to?"

Tamra directed him to a small diner a few minutes away from her office. They had decent food, fast service, and cozy seating for the two of them to catch up. The conversation was light and superficial on the way there. Tamra knew they'd be seeing how far down memory lane they could get in no time. An hour was hardly enough time with all the memories the two of them shared.

They were seated right away. Quinton leaned forward, clapped loudly and asked her what was new. Tamra just laughed and returned with a question.

"What are you doing here? You never said."

"Gran isn't doing well. They're not sure if she'll make it to Christmas so I needed to get out this way before, you know?"

"I'm sorry to hear that."

"Yeah…thanks. So," he paused. "How are you? Honestly?"

"Quint, it's crazy." She searched for the words to say. None of them came.

"I know what you mean," he saved her from her thoughts. "Financially, I'm doing better than I ever thought I would be. And, Chicago has no shortage of beautiful women. So I'm having lots of fun. But, I'm lonely."

Tamra gave him a face that clearly let him know she didn't believe him.

"I'm serious! Those women see a single, devastatingly handsome man that has something going for himself and want a sponsor. I'm ready to make an investment."

His tone let her know he was being honest. His eyes told her he was sad. His vulnerability touched her and proved that it was okay for her to tell him the truth. Before she knew it, she had told him just about everything and the food she had ordered but never touched was getting cold. Quint asked the waitress, who obviously hated her very existence, for a box, tipped her generously and led Tamra outside. That was the quickest hour of her life.

He pulled up outside her building and Tamra turned her head to avoid the group of people standing by the door smoking.

"The windows are tinted." They both laughed.

Tamra sighed aloud at the thought of going back into work. Her shoulders sagged because Quint was leaving just as soon as he had showed up.

"Come to Chicago for a few days."

"What?"

"Come to Chicago for a few days. You need to get away and I'd love for a visitor from home to come see me."

"I can't afford…"

"I didn't ask you what you could afford. Let's call it an investment."

Quint said he'd make arrangements for her to fly out on Friday night and be home early Sunday morning. All she had to do was say the word. She said she'd think about it. Tamra hopped out the car, trotted through the billows of smoke and bee lined for the handicap accessible bathroom that everyone used to take a dump. She threw her food in the trash can and called Dennise. She spoke softly into her cell phone so her voice wouldn't echo. Tamra barely got the story out of her mouth and her sister had agreed to watch Jayla for the weekend and offered her tips on how to blow Quint's mind in the bed.

Tam needed a sitter; however, one thing she and Quinton Davis never needed was sex tips. Now, she had to work up the nerve to fly out there and reopen a chapter that she never thought she'd be reading again.

Chapter 8

Tamra got settled in her seat and looked out the window. The flight attendant came by and asked if everything was okay for the millionth time. She just wanted to take off. The plane needed to get in the air before she backed out.

The week had flown by. Preparations to go see Quint almost seemed too easy. Tam felt like she was supposed to be doing this. Somehow, she knew that was her heart's way of overriding what her mind knew was right. She put her head back, closed her eyes and said a prayer. That's all she needed...something to happen to the plane and everyone at home would find out about her secret trip.

The October sky was already darkening over Harrisburg. Her flight landed at 9:11 p.m., Chicago time and Tamra knew she'd be exhausted by the time she got there. She hoped that Quint didn't try to take her on a tour of Chicago over the weekend. She just wanted to relax. The thought of him and relaxation made her smile.

Quint and Tamra knew each other in high school but didn't become close until they both attended college just outside of Philadelphia. They rode home together on breaks and he used her apartment as an underground railroad when he pledged. She couldn't pinpoint the moment that they had become friends. But, they had and Tamra couldn't have asked for a better one. People immediately speculated that they were sleeping together. So when they actually started, no one cared.

Tamra caught Hell over Quint. Girls on campus would befriend her to get close to him; then get jealous of their friendship. She always teased him about how hard it was to have him in her life. When they slept together for the first time, Tamra was so disappointed. It was then that she realized she hadn't had an orgasm before. That was until Quinton Davis did what Quinton Davis does. He completely and thoroughly pleased Tamra like she never thought was possible.

However, their bond was much deeper than a physical one. From wins to woes, to women…Quint told Tamra everything. In return she did the same. Their relationships sometimes suffered. They could detect a partner feeding them a line from a mile away. They both had an unfair advantage…each other.

That often worked against them as friends, though. Most people who knew them were baffled as to why they never dated seriously. Quint and Tamra knew the reason. They simply knew too much about each other. Furthermore, she knew she would hold every piece of information she had against him. The first sign of an argument, she would probably rattle off the name of every woman he had ever slept with. She'd even do it in chronological order.

The two hour flight gave Tamra ample time to think. About the rocky past; about the uncertain future. Most of all, about why on Earth she was on her way to Chicago at that present moment. Tamra told herself she wasn't running away from her problems at home. She was running into the arms of someone who would help her deal with them. Yeah…that's what this was.

She got off the plane and stepped into the airport. Everyone seemed to be in a rush. She stood there for a minute and took it all in. This was nothing like Harrisburg. After being bumped numerous times in ten seconds, Tamra realized she was in the way. She looked around for a sign to point her in the direction of baggage claims. She grabbed her suitcase and barely avoided falling onto and riding the conveyor belt. She navigated through the terminal as best as she could and was relieved when she saw the doors to exit.

Tamra walked a few feet and stood near a pillar. She leaned her suitcase against it and clutched her purse to her chest. Her eyes darted around in search of Quint. He insisted on picking her up. She told him she'd be fine catching a cab. But, when she saw how fast she would have to move to get in one, she was glad he persisted. The cool air whipped around her; making her pull her sweater tighter. They didn't call this place the Windy City for nothing!

It was just after 9:30 PM and it was already pitch black out. Tamra was tired, hungry and resisting the temptation to run back inside and fly home. She knew this was a bad idea. Maybe Quint had thought so too, and backed out.

"Where are you, Quint?" she whispered to herself.

"There you are, Girl! I've been looking all over for you."

He ran up to her and squeezed her tight.

"I thought you punked out on me," he teased.

She just laughed nervously. He grabbed her suitcase in one hand and interlocked his fingers with hers with the other. At first, Tamra was uncomfortable with that. Then she realized Quint was the only person in the city that she knew. Word would never get back to Joe Joe. Quinton pulled her into him and told her to keep up. He began to weave in and out of people and poles and trash cans at lightning speed. By the time they got to his car, Tamra was out of breath.

"Sorry about that, Babe. It's a little different than the 'Burg, huh?"

On the way to the house, they talked about the differences between Chicago and Harrisburg. Tamra was amazed at how Quint had seemed to adjust in the years he had been out there. It was as if he had lived there all his life.

Tamra peered out the passenger side window. She was half sightseeing and almost lost in her thoughts. The further they drove, the calmer things seemed to become. Quint turned down a long, dark road and only the blue tinted, halogen headlights of his Jaguar illuminated the street. They pulled up to an elaborate, wrought-iron gate. He punched a code in at the nearby keypad and it began to slide open. The townhouses in the gated community were gorgeous. They had stone fronts and identical lamp posts at the curb line. Each driveway had an expensive luxury car parked in it. Quint pulled into his driveway and hit the garage door opener to park. He ran around and opened her door for her then grabbed her luggage from the trunk. He seemed giddy that Tamra was actually there.

He unlocked and pushed the door open for her and she didn't move at first. His house was breathtaking.

"What's wrong?" he asked when she didn't move. She silently begged her feet to move.

Everything was cream and gold. Everything. Tamra immediately slipped her shoes off and lined them along the wall. She wanted to run her fingers along everything in the house. The décor was contemporary, but classic. She could tell he paid good money for everything but nothing was gaudy.

"I'm glad you're making yourself at home," he genuinely stated, pointing to her shoes.

"I just didn't want to get the carpet dirty."

"Tam, please! Don't act like that. I want you to be comfortable."

He led her to the living room and told her to have a seat on the oversized couch. He ran and took her luggage upstairs. The open floor plan allowed them to talk while he poured them some wine. He offered to heat up some barbeque wings. Her stomach growled but she declined for fear of spilling sauce everywhere. He handed her the wine glass and sat at the opposite end of the couch. She took several quick sips. They talked for a bit, kept drinking, and Tamra felt a buzz kicking in. She turned toward Quint and snuggled her feet in between the cushions of the couch. He leaned over and ran his hand up and down her leg.

"I am so happy you're here." He sounded sincere.

"Me, too." She was.

He stood up and put his hands out for her to take them. He helped her up and began guiding her to the steps.

"Tell me I'm the man," he said over his shoulder.

"What," she giggled.

"Just say it."

"You're the man," she said sarcastically.

"Keep saying it."

"You're the man…you're the man…you're the…"

Quint pushed his bedroom door open and Tamra gasped. There were candles everywhere. Rose petals were strewn about the floor. She could faintly hear 112 singing "Love You Like I Did". She didn't know what to do.

"Told you I'm the man."

He kissed her with a passion that made her swoon more than the alcohol. He ran his hands up and down her back. She ran hers along his head. He moaned aloud. She felt like she was melting into him. He kissed her on her forehead and led her into the master bathroom. There were candles lining the double counter and huge Jacuzzi tub. Rose petals floated on top of the water.

Quint began to undress Tamra. He softly kissed her skin, as it was exposed. He stood in front of her and planted kisses all over her neck and chest as he unhooked her bra with one hand. Tamra felt as light as a feather. Suddenly, he flicked on the bathroom lights.

"Tamra, what happened to you?" He asked horrified.

Gravity suddenly hit her again and the weight of what happened last week instantly laid upon her. Most of the stiffness and soreness had worn off so Tamra completely forgot about the bruises all over her back and torso. Being with Quint made Tamra forget about Joe Joe all together. She tried to cover the marks to no avail.

"What the Hell happened?" This time he demanded an answer.

"Joe Joe."

Fury flashed in his eyes and he stormed out of the bathroom. She stood there in just her underwear not sure of what to do next. They had ended up in the bathroom so fast that she never had a chance to warn him. And there's never really a good way to lead into telling someone your husband tried to beat you to a pulp. What ice breaker do you use just before that conversation?

For the first time since it happened, Tamra forced herself to look at the aftermath. She stared at the purple splotches on her caramel skin until tears made the colors run together. But, Tamra was tired of crying. And she was tired of how her life was going. Every time she allowed herself to smile, something happened to make her cry. She wasn't going to let that happen. At least, not this weekend.

She wiped her tears and went to find Quinton. She didn't have to look far. He was sitting on the edge of the bed with his head in his hands. She stood in front of him and caressed the waves in his hair.

"Why didn't you tell me, Tam?"

She had no verbal response to offer him. Instead, she placed his hands on her hips. She cupped his chin in hers and bent down and kissed his lips. His approach was soft like he was afraid to hurt her. She leaned in making him lay back on the bed. She straddled his hips and let her tongue meet his again. Quinton held her by her waist and flipped her over. With one hand he pinned her arms over her head. With just one finger of the other hand, he traced a line from her mouth, down the center of her body and stopped at the lace trim of her panties.

Tamra opened her eyes to see what had made him stop. He was looking at her like he had never seen her before. He began to kiss her bruises one by one. After each kiss, he said sorry. He apologized for not being there; for not protecting her. For all the pain she had been going through for months. A tear slipped from her eye and pooled in her ear.

She gently pushed him off of her and stood up. She pulled at her panties, stepped out of them, and walked into the bathroom. Quinton quickly followed. She stepped into the tub and lowered herself into the hot water. He hurried out of his clothes and got in behind her. He winced as the heat of the temperature controlled water touched his skin. He sat behind her and pulled her close to him. He did nothing to hide his arousal as he peeled rose petals off her and massaged her shoulders.

She spun around and ground her hips against his lap. With an effortless maneuver, he found her entrance and pushed inside of her. Her involuntary gasp was a mixture of pleasure and shock. Quint didn't move. Tamra found a slow and deep pace, letting him know she was okay. He rested his head on the back of the tub and she seized the opportunity to kiss his neck. That had always been his spot. In an effort to regain control, Quint gave her one long, hard thrust. Her scream echoed throughout the bathroom. Their movements caused water and roses to splash all over the floor.

They got out the tub and headed for the bedroom. Neither of them seemed concerned with the trail of water they were leaving behind. Tamra lay down across the bed. 112 was still on repeat. Quint caressed, kissed and stroked her so slowly. This was more than sex. He was telling her he loved her.

"Get up," she demanded. Quint obeyed.

Tamra turned over on all fours and arched her back. She had been thoroughly enjoying the lovemaking...a little too much. As if he read her tactic to prevent herself from falling for him, he slid back inside her and began to pound her into oblivion. Her screams drowned out all four of the men singing on the CD. She was sure she'd have a whole new set of bruises. That was a beating she was happy to take.

Chapter 9

Tamra woke up on Saturday morningcertain she had just been satisfied to the point of tears. She was totally confused about everything else. Questions bounced around in her head. She sighed heavily.

"Talk to me," She hadn't even noticed that Quint was awake. She just shook her head.

"Since when do you tell me no? Did I miss something?"

"Q…I…" She really didn't know.

"Tamra, I love you. And the biggest mistake I made with you was knowing you were different but not treating you like you were. I should have married you when I had the chance. I know you didn't expect all this. And I didn't expect to be saying it. But, I'm at a different place in my life. I just thought you needed to know."

His words were rushed, but sounded heartfelt. Tamra could feel his eyes burning a hole through her. She just kept staring at the ceiling. She hoped the words would appear for her to read to him. However, it looked like a piece of paper. Like her mind…blank.

Tamra cared for Quint. She honestly wanted him to be happy. He deserved that. She always knew that once he decided to settle down, he'd make some woman feel like a queen. Unfortunately, it couldn't be her. Not right now. It wouldn't be fair to him for her to even lead him to believe otherwise.

Fair. The mere thought of the word almost made Tamra laugh. If anything in life was fair, she wouldn't have gone through this much. So maybe Quint falling in love with her at a time when she couldn't be any more unavailable was his "fairness" to deal with.

Since she couldn't think of a nice way to relay her thoughts to him, she did the next best thing. She got up and walked out the room. She grabbed her cosmetic bag and went into the bathroom. She brushed her teeth and hopped in the shower. The scolding hot water hit her skin and caused steam to rise in plumes of smoke around her. She let it envelop her.

She could hear Quint come in, use the bathroom, run the water for awhile, and go back out. She wondered if she could just stay in the shower until it was time to catch her flight back home. When the water ran lukewarm, she knew she had to get out eventually and face him. Tamra had to give him some type of answer.

When she walked in the room, he was back in the bed. He smiled when she entered. It was contagious. She began to dig through her suitcase for clothes and he stopped her.

"Whatchuputtin' clothes on for?"

"I figured we'd be going out somewhere."

"You've got the city's finest attraction right here in this bedroom. I'll buy you a postcard with all the other ones at the airport."

She laughed and he pulled her onto the bed with him. They kissed and Tamra nestled herself in his arms. She felt so comfortable. For a second, she forgot that she had a life back in Pennsylvania; a tumultuous one, at that. But when their lips parted, it all came back to her. So she kept kissing him.

Time slipped away from them as they sexed each other for hours. The sun had emerged and retreated with them in each other's arms. Quint called the airline late Saturday night to get her on a Monday afternoon flight. Tamra had enough sick time that she could use. And neither of them was ready to leave each other's embrace.

They finally left the house, on Sunday evening, just in time to see the last gleam of sun disappear. Quinton had gotten them tickets to see Robin Thicke and Mary J. Blige and Tamra couldn't wait. She couldn't remember the last time she had been to a concert and Mary was one of her favorite artists.

They got to Millennium Park in time to get a decent parking space and an even better spot a few rows from the stage. Robin Thicke's voice was smooth as silk and Mary's performance was full of raw emotion. Mary sang the soundtrack of Tamra's life and Quint's arms were wrapped around her for every note. A slight gust of wind blew and Quinton pulled her tightly into him. He buried his face into her neck and kissed her gently. She smiled and inhaled the scent of his cologne.

Suddenly, they were bumped by someone and they turned to get an apology. A tall, thin, light skinned woman stood there. The sight of her made Quint pull away from Tamra. He obviously knew her. And she was obviously pissed to see Quint with Tamra.

"Hey, Quint.Funny seeing you here!" The beautiful woman spoke with a feigned cheerfulness and a smirk.

"Hey," Quint said flatly.

"I won't hold you up since you seem busy." She spoke over the music. "I was just wondering…did you find my panties from last week?" The music had gotten quiet but her voice hadn't. She purposely looked Tamra in the eyes. Everyone around them was now watching intently. Quint stood silent.

"Well if you do, just call me. You know how to find me. Enjoy your night!" And with that, she walked off.

"Tam," Quint sighed.

She put her hand up to dismiss anything he was getting ready to say. The intro to "Not Gon' Cry" started to play and Tamra batted away tears. Her efforts proved to be futile and her eyes became glassy and began to fill. She started to walk away but had no clue where she was going. But she knew she had to get away from everyone staring at her. Another gust of wind blew and seemed to tornado around her. She wished it would sweep her away.

Quint and Tamra rode back to his house in complete silence. He got right into the shower when they got in. Tamra turned on her cell phone for the first time since she got on the plane. She quickly ignored the several voicemail messages and searched the internet for a taxi company. She thought about leaving a note but didn't know what to say. She glanced around the room to make sure she had all of her belongings and pulled the bedroom door closed just as she heard Quint turn off the water.

Tamra stepped out into the brisk night air and walked quickly to the main gate. The wheels on her suitcase sounded loud enough to wake the dead. The rumbling sound echoed against the clear, black sky. She fumbled with the keypad to get out and slipped between the heavy gates as soon as they were open wide enough for her to get through. She looked up and down the street praying to soon see the headlights of a cab. She saw the headlights of a car pulling out of the development. The blue tint shined in Tamra's face and her heart pounded. Her regular beat resumed when she realized it wasn't Quint. The cab finally pulled up and she hopped in as fast as she could.

She slammed her head against the tattered leather seat. The cab driver tried to make small talk with her but quickly realized he was talking to himself. She decided to listen to her voicemails. They were all from Joe Joe. The first two were filled with apologies and regrets. One was laced with concern. The next three were hostile which Tamra assumed was from alcohol. And then there were a few hang ups.

When she got to the airport, she moved with purpose. She headed straight to the counter and all but sold her soul to the young girl working there to switch her ticket. By the time she was in the air, she had an indescribable headache. She had so much on her mind, her head felt like it would explode. She had left a troubled situation at home and flown right into another one. Now she was flying in the middle of the night back to the turmoil she left. She looked passed the man sleeping next to her and out the window at the pitch black sky. She felt like she was floating in a sea of nothingness.

Tamra almost felt foolish for being mad at Quint. She knew what kind of man he was and he had every right to be. She should have been mad at herself for believing his spiel in the bed earlier that morning. And she had no clue what condition she would find Joe Joe in when she got home. She didn't even want to go home. She figured since she was physically closer to God than normal, she would pray. She dropped her head, closed her eyes and gave the most heartfelt plea she could muster. She said amen and felt the plane rattle. The snoring senior citizen next to her jolted awake. The pilot came over the loudspeaker unnecessarily announcing that they were experiencing turbulence. *How fitting.*

After a layover that felt like an eternity, Tamra was exhausted by the time she got to Dennise's house just after 4:00 in the morning. She started to use her key when she noticed that the living room light was on. She gently pushed the front door open and startled Dennise and Eric.

"What the Hell," her sister yelled. Eric instinctively reached toward his hip.

"Nise, I'm sorry. I thought you'd be sleep. And I didn't know you'd have company while Jayla was here." Tamra's attitude was evident.

"Newsflash! This is my house. I can have who I want here whenever I want. You didn't ask no questions when you were hopping on the first thing smoking to cheat on your husband!" Eric giggled with squinted eyes.

"Are ya'll high?" Tamra shrieked. "Are you smoking weed with my child up in here?"

"Once again...my house. I do what I want. If you don't like it, you can leave and take your hyper child with you."

Tamra was livid but she couldn't go home. She couldn't wake Jayla at that time of night. She couldn't face Joe Joe. She headed for the steps lugging her suitcase behind her.

"Jayla's in the spare bedroom. Don't wake them kids up," Dennise called behind her.

Tamra slipped into the bedroom and stood over her peacefully sleeping daughter. Her heart swelled with love for her. Her brain throbbed from the thought of what she was putting her through. Tamra slowly lowered herself onto the bed in an effort not to wake her. She pulled her close. Jayla stirred a bit then fell soundly back to sleep. Tamra began to cry and waited for sunrise.

Chapter 10

Tamra awoke that Monday morning in a fog. She was already thrown off kilter because of the craziness of the weekend and waking up in a different bed. And between thinking and Quint's sporadic calls, she hardly slept a wink in those two hours since she got to Dennise's. By the time she had stayed out of the way as to not interrupt her sister's normal routine, and gotten Jayla dressed and to the car, she felt like she had already worked a full day.

"Mommy," Jayla's voice was soft. "Why don't you pray no more?"

"What are you talking about, Baby?"

"You don't pray no more. We used to pray in the morning and at night but you don't no more."

"Anymore," Tamra corrected her.

"Huh?" Jayla was confused by her answer.

"It's anymore. Not no more. And Mommy has been so busy and has a lot on her mind. Can you pray for me?"

"Sure!" Jayla began her sing-song version of the Lord's Prayer.

Tamra's mind had been so consumed that she couldn't remember the last time she stopped and prayed with Jayla. Tamra felt bad. She tried her best to shield her daughter. But, it was obvious that she knew something was wrong with Tam. Tam was finding it increasingly harder to keep her emotions in check and hide them from anyone lately. That definitely made her uneasy.

Tamra didn't feel like she had anything to hide; except for cheating on the husband that beat her up, of course. She felt like personal business should be kept personal. Her parents always taught her never to discuss problems with folks who don't have the solution. So Tam found herself talking to God. But, she didn't seem to be getting any answers.

"I said amen, Mommy," Jayla interrupted Tam's thoughts.

"Oh. Amen." Jayla just shook her head.

"Mommy, can we listen to Justin Bieber?"

Tamra happily popped the CD in and cranked it up to allow Jayla and the mop head phenomenon to drown out her stream of conscious.

Tamra dropped Jayla off at school and watched her skip across the street in the crosswalk. Her plaits bounced playfully and her smile was vibrant as she spotted one of her friends. Tamra would give anything to be that happy. Even if it was only for a moment.

When she got to work, it was as if God himself had hand-delivered that happiness in a vase and set it on her desk. Smack in the center of her work station was the most beautiful bouquet of flowers she had ever seen. There had to be at least 20 flowers in the bouquet and each of them were white. They were so bright. It seemed to mute all the other colors in the office.

"Is it your anniversary?" Shauna, her nosey coworker, asked.

"No, it's not."

"Hmph. Well, someone must love you. I googled those flowers. There are gardenias, hydrangeas, and two I can't pronounce. One starts with an L and the other one looks like the name Stephanie. And the ones with those little pink things sticking out the middle are Casablanca lilies. Somebody dropped some change on you, Ms. Tam!"

Shauna continued to chatter about how lucky Tamra was to have Joe Joe for a husband. She said any man that would spend that kind of money on flowers, just because, was in love. Tamra knew who they were from. The all white arrangement was a dead giveaway. She plucked the card from the middle of the bouquet and immediately began to dial Quint's number.

She knew she was wrong for leaving the way she did. He must have been worried sick since she hadn't answered any of his calls. She knew he was an hour behind but figured he'd at least be awake by now. She ran her finger along the top of the medium sized envelope, tearing it open. Quint answered the phone with a gravelly and sleepy voice.

"Quint, I just wanted to thank you for the beautiful...," She read the card and paused. The flowers were from Elijah.

"Hello?"

"Uh, weekend. Thank you for the beautiful weekend. Sorry I left the way I did. Call me when you wake up."

"Tamra, are you okay? I've been calling you since you left. You keep ignoring my calls. Now, you're rushing me off the phone?" He was irritated and she could tell.

"I'm sorry. I just wanted to let you know I'm still alive. Call me later and we'll talk." She hung up.

Tamra read the card over and over. Her eyes traveled from the words to the flowers and back again.

Tamra,

I wanted to send you flowers that are as beautiful as you are. But, none of the colors did your beauty any justice. Each time you look at these white flowers, may they cause you to flash your sparkling smile. I want to get to know you. Please call me.

~Elijah

She swiped her cell phone from her desk and clutched the card for dear life. Once outside, she dialed nine numbers and stopped before punching in the last one. She quickly hit the last number and prayed he wouldn't answer. He did.

"Elijah McCall," he sounded like a salesman.

"Hi, Elder McCall. It's Sister Jordan."

"Hey, Tamra! It's so good to hear from you."

"I, uh, was, uh, calling to say thank you for the flowers. They are absolutely beautiful."

She looked around to see if anyone could hear her. There were a few people rushing inside the building to punch in on time. No one seemed to be paying her any attention.

"Well, uh, you're, uh, very welcome," he teased and it made her laugh.

"I can't talk long but again, I just wanted to say thanks."

"When will you be able to talk long?" His voice turned serious.

"Elder McCall, I…"

"Elijah," he corrected her.

"Elijah, I told you I'm married."

"And if I had any questions about your status, I would have asked you that. But I asked about your schedule."

"Oh," Her eyebrows shot up. Tamra was taken aback by his brazen comment.

"I'll tell you what, whenever you do have some time to talk to me, please let me know." He had lightened up. "I really want to get to know more about you."

"Well, I'll tell YOU what. I'll text you my email address and we can start from there. You have a blessed day."

He just chuckled before hanging up. She immediately sent him a text message and headed back upstairs to her desk. She started to work, but couldn't resist the urge to open her personal email in case he decided to email her right away. She decided not to reply to his first one immediately, though. She didn't want to seem eager. She didn't even know why she encouraged him to email her.

There was something about Elijah. It had only been a few weeks since they first laid eyes on each other. When he looked at her, she felt like he knew more than the little she had told him. Maybe that's why she was going along with this. She wanted to know how much he knew and who had told him. She couldn't deny that she was physically attracted to this man. There was an intrigue in his eyes that pulled her in.

After taking a few calls and hitting her send/receive button a million times, Tamra got an email from Elijah. He thanked her for allowing him to email her. He said he was happy that she liked the flowers. He ended the email with the same request he had been giving her. He asked her to tell him about herself. He wanted to know more about her.

Elijah,

I'm married and the mother of two daughters. I work for an insurance brokerage firm. I've been attending Bible Tabernacle for a short time but I enjoy it a lot. I have one brother and one sister and I've lived in Harrisburg all my life. What else would you like to know?

~Tamra

She hit send and nervously rapped her fingers on her desk. Time began to move in slow motion. By the time lunch time rolled around, Tamra couldn't wait to get out of the building. She decided to drive home, put her luggage in the house and grab a bite to eat.

She was relieved when she pulled into the empty driveway. It meant that Joe Joe wasn't home and she had avoided confronting him for a little while longer. She opted not to pull into the garage since she'd be in and out. Her neighbor's front door flung open as she pulled her suitcase from the trunk and Tamra immediately regretted that decision.

"I was wondering where you were. I was starting to get worried."

Ms. Geri was recently widowed, but probably didn't notice yet because she was always so busy minding everyone else's business.

"I'm still alive, Ms. Geri. Thanks." Tamra tried to move quickly since the lady was walking across Tam's front lawn.

"Well, where did you go? And where's Baby Girl?" Tamra spun around on her heels and looked the woman dead in her eyes.

"Ms. Geri." She took a deep breath before continuing. "I only have a few minutes before I have to be back to work. Maybe you can ask me all the questions you want some other time."

Ms. Geri seemed insulted and headed back to her house. Tamra fumbled with the key and kicked the front door open. She dropped her keys on the small table just inside the door. Before she could do anything else, the door flew shut and banged against her bag that wasn't even all the way in the house. She felt a massive hand grab hold of her braided ponytail and yanked with such a force that she thought her hair had been ripped out at the root. She heard his voice before she saw him but she immediately knew it was him.

"Where the fuck you been?"

Joe Joe was irate…and drunk. She didn't see him hiding behind the door. She screamed as he threw her to the ground. Not again. He straddled her across her chest and his thighs made it hard for her to breathe. But she did. And screamed and fought. He wasn't going to beat her behind uncontested this time. He would earn every blow. He grabbed her by her collar and repeatedly asked her where she had been. He shook her violently, causing her head to bang on the floor and the buttons of her shirt to pop off.

Tamra clinched her eyes closed and flailed her fists at Joe Joe. She connected several times but he was unfazed. She had to get him off of her. If she let him slam her head into the hardwood floor again, she'd surely die of severe head trauma. He leaned in close to her. She opened her eyes, looked this monster in the face and then clawed at his eye with all her might. Her fingertips bore into his bottom eyelid and he let out a blood curdling howl. Tam dug deeper. It was her intent to rip the side of his face clear off. He rolled off of her and onto his back. She kicked him between his legs like she was punting a football in the Super Bowl and the game was on the line. He screamed again and she ran out the front door, nearly breaking her neck as she tripped over her bags.

Ms. Geri came bounding out of her house again. This time, she was yelling into her cordless phone.

"There's an intruder," she shrieked. "He's killing her!" She kept repeating the address.

Sirens blared and Harrisburg police vehicles swarmed the block. The first few officers ran into the house with their guns drawn. Another one ran to Tamra as Ms. Geri pointed in her direction. The middle aged, olive skinned man rapidly fired off questions at Tamra. He kept asking her to describe the intruder. He wanted as much information as possible. But, Tamra didn't know that man.

"He's 6'3"," Tamra held her shirt closed. "Brown skinned, low hair cut, goatee." She rubbed her own face with her free hand.

"You're doing great, ma'am. Is there anything else you can tell me about him?"

"He's my husband," she said softly.

"Excuse me?" His expression and tone proved that he had heard what Tamra said. He just didn't believe that she had said it.

"Joseph Jordan. He's sick. He started drinking after our daughter died a few months ago." Tamra said these things as if she was pleading for mercy on Joe Joe's behalf.

The policemen that had run into the house walked out announcing that all was clear. Tamra began to breathe heavily. She wondered where Joe Joe had gone.

"Do you know where your husband may have gone?" She shook her head no and just stared off into nowhere. She swiped away tears that hadn't stopped falling since she walked in her house.

Two female officers escorted Tamra inside to change her shirt. She repeatedly denied medical attention. She felt so awkward with the women in her bedroom. She wanted to crawl in her bed but the girls in blue stood there with their hands resting on their Tasers. Lying down was unlikely. She led them downstairs and noticed that everything in the living room was untouched. Besides the scuff marks on the floor, it seemed the altercation never occurred. Tamra took the business card from a questioning officer, grabbed her keys and headed back to work.

"I'll be sure to call the poh-lice again if he shows up here, okay?" Ms. Geri yelled at Tamra as she backed out of the driveway.

She got back to work and felt like a zombie walking back to her desk. She lifted the vase up and put it underneath her work station. They were the complete opposite of her life. She had no room for beauty right now. As if on cue, her own personal beast called her office phone. Too bad she hadn't paid any attention to the caller ID before answering.

Joe Joe was sobbing so loudly on the other end. He asked her why she made him act like that. Why didn't she just answer him? Tamra became enraged.

"How dare you? How dare you blame me? I told you the first time you tried to beat me to death, you need help. I don't know where you are. But you can stay your black ass there until you get some."

"That house is just as much mine as it is yours. I'll be back in a few days." He hung up on her. She called a locksmith.

Chapter 11

Tamra went home that night and stepped inside the front door with caution. She rushed Jayla through dinner and ushered her right upstairs to the master bedroom. Jayla didn't put up much of a fight since she always begged Tamra to sleep in her room with her. Tamra locked the door behind them and tried to settle in for the night. Surprisingly, she fell right to sleep.

She woke up Tuesday morning almost embarrassed at herself. She had the most vivid and erotic dream of her life. It was about Elijah. She shook Jayla to wake her and hoped she hadn't heard Tamra talking or moaning in her sleep. If Jayla had heard, she didn't let on but Elijah must have read her mind. He sent her a text. He bid her a good morning, not knowing he had already given her a great night. She text him back and proceeded to get dressed. They talked the entire morning and Tamra found herself smiling the entire time. While at her desk, her cell phone rang. She was disappointed that it wasn't Elijah. It was Joe Joe's brother.

"Hello, Ricky." She didn't hide her disappointment.

"Tam," he sounded tired. "How long you gon' make this man suffer?"

Tamra pulled the phone away from her ear and looked at it. Her ears had to be deceiving her so she was relying on her eyes. No, she had seen the right name the first time.

"Ricky, I'm not sure what your brother has told you but I can assure you, he's not the one suffering in this situation." She heard her phone vibrate. "And furthermore, whatever happens between me and Joe Joe should stay between me and Joe Joe. I apologize for you being drug in the middle of this but I'd appreciate it if we end this conversation now."

"Listen here, Tam. That's my brother. He showed up at my house yesterday and said he needed me. So I'm going to be there for him. But, I thought you needed to know that he wants to work this out. He needs us, Tam." Her phone vibrated again.

"What he needs is an alcoholic's anonymous meeting. I don't have any of those lying around the house; but, I wish him well finding one. What I can help with is some clean clothes. You can stop by the house and get a bag for him. They will be by the front door tomorrow morning."

There was silence for a few seconds. Ricky was obviously waiting for her to continue. She was waiting for him to realize that there was nothing more to discuss.

"Fine, Tamra."

She quickly hung up so she could read the texts from Elijah. The first one asked if he could see her soon. The second one said: "I guess that means no." She apologized for not responding right away and spent the rest of the day and night texting and talking to him on the phone.

Wednesday morning came and brought butterflies with it. She couldn't wait to get to bible study. She felt like she hadn't been to church in forever and she couldn't wait to see Elijah. She knew she just had to get through the day.

Tamra walked over to Joe Joe's drawer and pulled out several pairs of socks and boxers. She grabbed some uniform shirts and a pair of pants from the closet. She folded everything up and carefully placed it all in his gym bag. She packed all the essentials he needed and sat down next to the bag.

The last time she had packed a bag for Joe Joe, they were taking a family vacation to the beach. That was just a few months ago. They needed to get away. Tamra had hoped it would reconnect the three of them. He had just started becoming very distant and she thought the trip would do them all some good. And it did; for a short time. However, soon after they got home, he retreated further into his isolation. Even as bad as Tamra thought it was, she never thought it would ever get here.

Tamra had lost sight of the small steps that occurred along the road to this personal Hell. The journey back to some sense of normalcy seemed impossible. She would just have to create a new one. As the time went on, it was becoming more evident that it would be without Joe Joe. With the way things were going, she just wanted to pack up, drive away and start over with nothing but Jayla in the car.

Jayla jumped in the back seat of the car and started to pray. Tamra made sure to join in. Amen was barely out of her their mouths when Jayla started to question Tam.

"Mommy?" Based on the way she said it, Tamra braced herself for what was coming next.

"Yes, Jay Jay?"

"Is Daddy getting a new house?" Tamra adjusted the rearview mirror to look at her. She was concentrating on whatever game she was playing on her Nintendo DS.

"Why would you ask me something like that?"

"Because you put his clothes outside," Jayla said matter-of-factly.

"No, Sweetie. He's going to go to the gym at lunch. I put his clothes by the door so he could just grab the bag and go. Mommy put cool clothes in there for him. You know how Daddy dresses." Tam gave her a fake laugh.

"Oh," was Jayla's only response.

Tamra's day was sailing by. She was on the phone with an insurance agent, when Megan came and stood by her desk. Tamra signaled to her that she would only be a moment. Megan whispered for her to take her time. Tamra turned her back to her and rolled her eyes. After her phone call ended, Megan asked Tamra to follow her back to her office.

When they got there, Tam shut the door behind her, sat down, took a deep breath, and prepared herself for what was coming next.

"Tamra, the managers' team is thoroughly impressed with you." Her eyebrows shot up. Tam wasn't sure if she was supposed to respond or wait for more.

"Well, thank you, Megan."

"We have discussed re-vamping the case management training process." Another pause.

"Okay?" Tamra wished she'd just spit it out.

"Are you interested in being a trainer?"

Tamra hadn't even seen that coming.

"Of course, I'm interested! I'm sure there are some particulars you all need to work out. So when you have everything figured out, let me know and I'll review the offer."

"Ummm, right!Particulars, yeah." Apparently they hadn't thought that far ahead.

"Sounds good. Just let me know when you all are ready to talk."

Tamra headed back to her desk. As she walked by Shauna, she heard her telling someone she had just gotten back to her desk.

"I'll transfer you right now." Tam answered her phone before even sitting down.

"American Insurance Services. This is Tamra. How can I help you?" Tam bent over the back of her chair and grabbed a pen and some paper to take notes.

"Hi, Sister Jordan! It's Tawonda."

Tamra wanted to ask her what the Hell she wanted and how the Hell she knew where she worked. But, like most busy bodies, Tawonda voluntarily offered the information on her own.

"I hope I'm not interrupting you on your job. I got your company name from your file in the new members' class and I Googled the number." Tamra wrote down the number that appeared on the caller ID and sat down. Tawonda continued talking.

"I'm starting a clothing bank for the less fortunate and was wondering if you would be willing to donate your dead daughter's clothes since you're not using them. I'd appreciate it if you could bring them to bible study tonight. Or will you be skipping church again?"

Tamra had never wanted to kill someone. At that moment however, she could visualize taking Tawonda's life. How could someone who had no reason to hate her say such vile things? She couldn't think of a reason to make anyone hate another person that much at all. She couldn't even think at the moment. She slammed the phone so hard, she had possibly ruptured Tawonda's ear drum, instantly causing her to go deaf. Tamra could only hope.

Tamra got home later than evening still fuming from Tawonda's call. She went to the door leading to the basement, put her hand on the knob and inhaled deeply. She held the oxygen in her chest and practically ran through Joe Joe's man cave. She got to the door to the storage room and gave it a push for it to open. She exhaled and breathed rapidly as if she had been under water after she shut the door behind her. She walked over to the one bin that she hadn't opened since she closed it months before.

It was like opening a time capsule. Kya's clothes smelled the same. There were only a few items left. Everything else had burned along with her. Tamra managed to save a load of laundry that was in the basement when the house caught fire. She pulled out each item one by one and held them close to her chest. She quickly pulled them away from her. She didn't want her perfume to get on the clothes.   Maybe it was time for her to get rid of them. As much as it pained her to even think it, Tawonda was right. She wasn't using them. And maybe keeping them in a dark corner in the basement was preventing her from moving on. Getting rid of the clothes didn't mean she was getting rid of the memory of Kya. The clothes would be going to a family that could really use them. Then both families would benefit. Maybe Tawonda wasn't all bad after all.   *Screw that hoe.* Tamra snapped the lid back on the tote and slid it back to its spot. She ran upstairs and rushed Jayla along so they could make a stop on the way to bible study. Jayla complained the whole way there. She hated not knowing where Tam was taking her. But, Tam was in no mood to deal with her whining. She pulled into the Target parking lot and practically drug Jayla in the store by her little arm. She hopped in the shortest line she saw, pulled a gift card off the display and asked for $50 to be loaded onto it. She stuffed the card and the receipt in her purse and drug poor Jayla back out the store.

Tamra marched into the church with her eyes set for her target. Tawonda. She gave a few members quick hugs and short hellos and no explanation for her brief absence. Her internal radar started going off and she headed for Tawonda. Tamra stood over top of her as she sat at the end of a pew talking to another church member. Tamra ignored the other woman's excitement to see her. She flicked the gift card at Tawonda and it boomeranged toward her throat. Tawonda jumped just before she got a paper cut to the jugular.

"That's the contribution from me and my dead daughter."

Tamra went straight to the altar and knelt down to pray.

Chapter 12

The next evening, Tamra found herself walking back through the doors of the church again. But, this time she wasn't angry. When she had prayed, she sincerely asked for forgiveness. And when she got up, she let the anger stay there. God could handle it better than she could, anyway.

In her haste to leave bible study the night before, Tamra had left her bible and a bag with her mail on the pew. Some of the ladies were already there having a missionary meeting so she decided to pop in and grab it. Tamra was looking forward to a relaxing night once she made it back home. Dennise had picked Jayla up from school to take her skating with the kids.

Tamra tried to look for her bag and bible without interrupting the meeting in progress. No such luck. Sister Adams immediately spotted her and drew everyone's attention to her.

"I'm so sorry, Ladies! I'm just looking for my bible that I left here last night." She whispered.

"That's quite alright, Tammy!" Sister Adams had called Tamra every variation of her name except the right one since she met her. "Look in the bin in the overflow room. That's the lost and found box." She broke out into laughter. Tamra wasn't sure why. She hurried out of the room so they could continue their meeting.

When Tam got to the adjacent room, she didn't see a bin anywhere. She looked all over and decided to look in the Sunday school rooms. She walked into the first room just as she noticed that people were in there talking. Tamra started to apologize and realized it was Tawonda and Elijah. They were holding hands praying. Then she saw her things. She tried to grab her bag and hurry out undetected. She failed again. Tamra quickly apologized for intruding and explained why she was there in the first place. Both sets of eyes fell upon her. Elijah's danced with excitement. Tawonda's shot bullets at her.

"Again, I'm sorry."

"No worries," Elijah said. "We were just wrapping up."

"Elder McCall, I'd be happy to take you home." Tawonda turned her back to Tamra but spoke loud enough for her to hear.

"No, thank you. Sister Jordan will take me." He looked right past Tawonda and directly into Tamra's eyes.

"I sure will, Elder. You're not far from me."

Tawonda turned and followed Elijah's gaze. If looks could kill...

Once inside the car, they both seemed to relax a little. Tamra turned the volume of the CD player down as Trey Songz belted out "Does he do it like I do it." Elijah finished the lyrics. She looked at him in shock.

"There you go again. How come you can listen to Trey but I can't?" They both laughed.

"I appreciate the ride."

"I was surprised you didn't take Tawonda up on her offer," she teased. "You know that girl wants you, right?"

"I can neither confirm nor deny what that girl wants," he threw his hands up to prove his innocence.

"Yeah, right," she responded sarcastically.

"Plus, it doesn't matter what she wants. I want you. And you want me."

Tamra adjusted her seatbelt which suddenly felt like it was getting tighter. She turned the music back up. Elijah just shook his head and chuckled. After a minute of neither of them talking, he turned the music back down.

"If I'm not mistaken, you were one of the ones who committed to making sure I got a home cooked meal while I'm up here. What's with tonight? I'm hungry."

Before Tamra knew it, she was on Derry Street headed to her house, instead of his hotel. She quickly parked and ushered him in the house past Joe Joe's bag and nosey eyes. Unfortunately, Tamra noticed that he had noticed both the bag and her discomfort. Elijah walked in and sat on the couch like he lived there. That struck Tamra as odd. He knew she was married. How did he know Joe Joe wasn't there? Her cell phone rang, interrupting her mental questions. It was Quint. She ignored the call and Elijah's quizzical stare. She sat down in the chair instead of sitting on the couch with Elijah.

"So, what's your favorite food?" She asked.

"I'd settle for anything you have in there. I'm just tired of eating out."

"That's not what I asked you. What's your favorite food?"

"Thai chicken. Since I doubt you have any of that lying around, I'll take anything you got." She got the feeling he was talking about more than chicken.

"I'll see what I can whip up." She looked over her shoulder and caught him watching her hips sway.

Tamra ignored another call from Quint and pulled up Google on her cell phone. She prayed she had the ingredients to make Thai chicken, or something close to it, as the recipe loaded. She scrolled through them and smiled when she saw she had everything needed to make coconut chicken. Even the coconut milk. Her experimental cooking was paying off. She scored the chicken and laid it in the milk, tomato sauce and ginger concoction. She washed her hands and poured Elijah a tall glass of orange tea cooler. He was playing with his phone. She gave him the remote control and told him she'd be right back.

Once back in the kitchen, she wrapped the chicken breasts in aluminum foil with diced vegetables. She figured baking the chicken instead of pan searing it would give her some more time with Elijah. She grabbed some juice for herself and went and sat in the living room with him. He patted the cushion next to him for her to come closer. She did so with no hesitation.

"What was your favorite game to play when you were little?" He waited for her answer.

"What kind of question is that," Tamra asked.

"I wanna know. Just answer the question," he pleaded.

Tamra looked into the air to search her past. She smiled when her mind conjured the mental picture.

"Barbies."

"Why," he pressed.

She sat her glass down on the end table so she could talk with her hands.

"I could create the world I wanted to live in. I had the house, the Corvette, the camper, all the Barbie clothes and, of course, Ken." Her voice dropped off a bit. "When I grew out of playing with Barbies, I tried to live that life for real. But, things are different outside that beach house. What about you?"

Elijah set his glass down and leaned into her. She could smell his cologne. She took deep breaths to take it in.

"Why are you so determined to keep me out?"

"You're sitting on my couch, watching my television, drinking my juice and about to eat some of my food. How much more *in* do you want to be?"

"All the way." He laid his head on her shoulder and locked his eyes onto Tamra's. She felt herself falling into the two small pools of chestnut brown. She wanted to dive head first into him.

"What is it about me, Elijah?"

He smiled like he had been waiting for her to ask.

"You…are…beautiful." He spoke slowly as if he wanted those words to seep into her belief. "You have an eagerness in your eyes that is undeniable. You haven't been jaded by years of religion but you want to learn. You're human. You listen to Trigga Trey on your way to bible study." She broke out into a huge smile. "And that wrinkle in your nose when you smile is too cute for words."

He kept listing things he liked about her. Things that intrigued him.She hadn't even realized that he noticed so much about her. But he did. Habits, mannerisms, and things she thought she hid. Elijah seemed to see them all. And he recited them to her like a Shakespearian sonnet. She wanted him to talk forever.

But, it seemed he wanted to use his lips in another capacity. He slowly leaned in to kiss her and showed the slightest hint of hesitation. She proceeded to let him know it was okay. Tamra's lips touched Elijah's. She had been imagining that moment since the first time she saw them. They were softer than she thought they would be. How was that even possible? She parted her lips just wide enough to let his tongue slide between them. She turned her body toward him and placed her hand on his face. The harshness of his manicured beard met her fingertips. She lightly scratched and tugged at the hair on his face. He remained still, totally concentrated on the effect his kiss was having on her.

She wanted him to take control but he only kept kissing her. His body leaned, head tilted, doing nothing but kissing her. Yet, she felt like he was touching every part of her. Tamra had never been kissed like this before. They stopped for a second and he gave her a quick peck on the lips. But, the fire he had ignited in her wouldn't die down. So she pulled him for another deep, passionate embrace. This time, he returned it. She could feel the muscles in his arms flex as he tightened his grip around her. She put one of her legs on the couch behind him and lay; back pulling him with her. The heat between them was indescribable.

Tamra slipped her foot out of her shoe and raised the leg that had been planted on the floor up. She started a trail up his leg and into his lap. She got midway up his thigh and the smoke alarm in the dining room began to blare. The sound nearly gave Tamra a heart attack. She pushed Elijah off of her and ran into the kitchen. They had been talking and wrapped in each other's arms so long, she totally forgot she had food in the oven. She turned the dial on top of the stove off, grabbed a nearby hand towel and fanned the smoke that was pouring out. After fanning the smoke detector to silence the deafening sound, she went into the kitchen and pulled the pan of smoldering aluminum foil pouches out of the oven. Only the bottom of the chicken was burnt but the vegetables were a lost cause.

She stood at the counter and wanted to cry. Her chest was heaving from panic. Smoke alarms did that to her. She hadn't heard Elijah walk into the kitchen, but the sensation of him standing so closely behind her started to calm her down a bit. He turned her around and just hugged her. She laid her head on his chest. The rapid pace of her heart slowed down from being held by him. She heard the beat of his heart quicken from having her in his arms.

"You okay?" He asked with genuine concern in his voice.

"I will be."

He tilted her head toward his and kissed her gently and hugged her tight. He pulled away, kissed her forehead and continued to hold her. She could have fallen asleep standing up in his arms. Instead, she tried to pull herself back together.

"I'm so sorry about burning the food." She was a tad bit embarrassed. She started to peel the chicken breasts off the pan and throw them away.

"Whatchu doing, Babe? I'm gon' eat that."

She looked at him in disbelief.

"Elijah, the bottom is burnt. You can't eat that!"

"Well, I'll eat the top." He shrugged.

"Wow. You really haven't had a good meal in a while, huh?"

"It's not that. I just appreciate the effort you put into making it for me. I understand that you can't cook." He poked fun at her.

They both peered at the clock at the same time and noticed it was getting late.

"I know you have to go get Baby Girl. So, can I get this to go?"

Tamra sensed disappointment in his voice. She was disappointed, too. She cut off the burnt pieces of chicken and wrapped it up. She put some leftover spaghetti in a plastic container and placed the food in a bag for him. They walked out the front door chatting and giggling when Ms. Geri's front porch light flicked on. Tamra sighed heavily. Just as expected, her front door flew open. Tamra just continued toward the car.

"Well, hello neighbor!" Ms. Geri called from her porch. Tamra just waved. "And hello to your gentleman friend."

"How are you, Ma'am," Elijah asked pausing before getting in the car. Tamra cringed. Ms. Geri was surprised that he responded to her. She was at a loss for words when he left the car door open walked toward her.

"It's a beautiful night out, isn't it?" Elijah stopped just short of going up her steps. Ms. Geri nodded. He kept talking. "These are beautiful flowers you have here. Did you plant them yourself?" She nodded again. He still kept talking. Tamra wanted to kill him. "Well, I guess you've gotten a good look at me by now. You have a good night, okay?" Ms. Geri rushed back into her house. Tamra's mouth fell open. Elijah just started laughing.

Tamra dropped Elijah off and called her sister. They were at Dennise's house and as usual, she sounded like she had an attitude when Tam called. When she pulled up, Dennise sent Jayla out the front door without even giving Tamra a chance to get out the car. Jayla jumped in the back seat and said, "Aunt Nise said you owe her twenty dollars. Tamra laid her foot on the gas and peeled off.

Chapter 13

The next afternoon, Tamra headed to her appointment with her therapist. It had felt like forever since she had been there. A lot had happened since her last visit and Tamra had no plans on telling Dr. Steele about any of it. But, Tamra's constant shifting in her chair told it for her. Dr. Steele asked her a few questions and she answered them less than satisfactorily. Instead, she tried to ask the questions.

"Dr. Steele, is it possible to be in love with multiple people?"

"Do you think you are?"

"I'm just asking," Tamra's eyes roamed around the room.

"Well, Tamra, I'd prefer that we stay on topic. How about we discuss things that are specific to you. Have you been journaling everyday?"

"Not everyday. I've been pretty busy lately. Let me ask you this, though. How long after the end of one relationship do you think a person should wait before beginning a new one?"

"Tamra, I know I left you with a pretty heavy question the last time we met. And I hoped you would give that question some serious thought. But, it seems that you are not ready for it. And to be perfectly honest with you, it's a waste of both of our time to continue this session until you are ready." Dr. Steele seemed extremely irritated. She set her pen and notepad on her desk and walked toward the door.

"I'll let my secretary know that there is no need to schedule an appointment for next week. Feel free to give the office a call when you are ready to resume. Have a good day."

Tamra gathered her things and slowly walked by Dr. Steele. She wasn't sure what to say so she said nothing at all. She bid the young woman at the front desk farewell and picked up her pace as she exited the office. Tamra went back to work spent the afternoon emailing Elijah and ignoring a few more calls from Quint. She checked her voicemails as she walked out of work and he had hung up on each of them. She knew she would have to call him some time. But, now wasn't it. Her phone rang again as she got in her car and she assumed it was from him again. But, it was from her sister. The outcome was still the same. Tamra wasn't in the mood to talk to her either so she sent her straight to voicemail. Tamra figured she only wanted to argue anyway.

Tamra's mind was full and her thoughts slammed into each other. She didn't have to pick Jayla right up after school so she decided to make a trip to the cemetery. She turned left onto Lincoln Street and proceeded up the narrow Steelton road. When she got to the top of the hill, she stopped. She thought about turning around and going home but someone had pulled up behind her and beeped their horn for her to get out of the way.

She parked in the same spot she always did. It was between the granite bench and the large weeping willow tree. Kya was buried in the middle of the two. The autumn wind blew gently causing the branches of the tree to droop with sadness. Tamra sat on the white bench and felt the coldness of the stone on the back of her legs. She took a few deep breaths before going to Kya's tombstone.

Tamra wiped leaves away from the grave marker. They were brittle and crunched between her fingers. She straightened the arrangement of flowers that were in the cast iron vase. Joe Joe had probably been there recently. He had made sure flowers were on her grave since she was buried. Tamra immediately began to pray.

She prayed for Joe Joe. As mad as she was at him, she knew that wasn't him. He was slowly dying. She prayed that he would stop drinking and learn to deal with the fact that Kya was gone. It was as if he wouldn't accept it. She prayed for Jayla. Tam knew that she had to be suffering just as much as everyone else. But, she didn't show many signs of it. Tamra knew that those feelings would manifest themselves sooner or later. And finally, Tamra prayed for herself. She had never been so confused in her life. She couldn't bring herself to have divorce papers drawn up. She had flown half way across the country to sleep with another man. And she was quickly falling for a man that she knew next to nothing about. The web of her life seemed to be wrapping tightly around her. She grabbed a water bottle from the car and filled it with water at a nearby water fountain. She filled the vase, ran her fingers across Kya's name, blew her a kiss and headed back to the car.

Two days later, Tamra was in full mommy mode. It was Saturday morning and she was running on her usual weekend schedule...late. Jayla had a soccer game and they both scurried around the house trying to get ready. Just as she had made a little progress, she got a text from Elijah. It stopped her dead in her tracks. It didn't say anything significant. But the fact that he was thinking of her meant more than she could comprehend. And that scared Tamra. Elijah had quickly and effortlessly worked his way into her thoughts and consumed every moment of them. When she wasn't talking to him, she was thinking about when she would be talking to him again. Tamra was almost embarrassed about how smitten she was by him. If she didn't know any better, she would think that she was falling for him.

She snapped from her far off gaze when Jayla busted in the room hopping on one foot trying to pull her hot pink shin guard up. Tamra shook her head and smiled at her daughter. She had signed Jayla up for soccer in order for her to make some new friends and to release some of the extra energy she seemed to always have. Jayla was all for the idea at first. She had a blast picking out migraine pink accessories and modeling them throughout the house before her first game. And two minutes after the first whistle blew, Jayla was over it. Since then, it had been a hassle getting her to practices and games. But, Tamra was determined to make her stick with it at least until the end of the season. Neither of them could wait until that time came.

Tamra gathered everything she needed and ran downstairs and poured herself a cup of steaming coffee to go. Habit led her to the basement door. She had opened it and listened for evidence of Joe Joe being there before she realized how long it had been since he had even been in the house. Her heart unexpectedly dropped a little. She was relieved that he wasn't there because of their last encounter. But, she couldn't help but to think that even the distant, drunk shell of a man she once loved was better than the deafening silence in the basement. She shooed Jayla out the door and scooped up the newspaper that was laying on the front stoop.

They pulled up just as Jayla's team was dispersing from their huddle and scattering onto the field. Jayla took off to join them looking like a blur of pink and plaits whizzing by. Tamra grabbed her purse, newspaper, cup of liquid energy and headed toward her usual spot among the other parents. She got half way there before she realized she had forgotten her fold up chair. She doubled back, grabbed it from the trunk, and added it to the items she was balancing. She knew that once she got settled she'd only have to make small talk for an hour and then she could go on about her day. She greeted the other moms and Chase's permanently perky mother immediately started to ramble on. Tamra pretended to care.

"Hi, Jayla's mom! It's pretty cool out here today. I brought snacks for after the game for everyone. Does Jayla like apple juice?"

Tamra gave her a few nods and eyebrow raises to make her think she was paying attention. The woman didn't seem to need any response, though. The sound of her own voice satisfied her. Tamra spotted her sister and Eric sitting across the field on the bleachers watching their kids who were on the opposing team. She started to go and sit with them to avoid the "Chatty Cathy" but figured that would be like moving from one headache to another. She waved to them and decided to stay put. She got comfortable and started to open the newspaper when Quinton appeared out of nowhere.

"So you're just going to ignore me, Tamra? For real?"

His large frame cast a shadow over her. The fact that he was standing there made her freeze. The other parents looked on in disbelief and didn't hide their interest in the unexpected show.

"Quinton, what? Oh my God. What are you doing here?" She looked around to see who was watching. Everyone.

"I can't even believe you!" His voice was loud but shaking.

She had never seen him like this. He moved closer to her. One of the fathers took a step toward them. Quinton shot him a look that made him instantly retreat. Embarrassment washed over her. He did not seem to care that all attention was on them. He continued to fire statements at her about how insensitive she was. The game had come to a complete halt. Jayla was running toward them. She glanced back at Dennise again who smirked as Eric pulled her in close to him. Tamra hurriedly grabbed her things and raced toward her car with Jayla trotting closely behind her.

She threw the barely folded chair into the back seat with her daughter as it banged her in the leg.

"M-o-o-o-o-m!" Jayla acted as if Tamra had sawed the leg off.

"Not now, Jay Jay!"

Tamra tossed the newspaper off of her purse and dug inside of it to grab some Advil. She popped two in her mouth and they were half swallowed before she gulped the now lukewarm coffee. She buried her face into her hands and waited for the throbbing to begin. It didn't take long. She couldn't believe what had just happened. She wanted to kill Quint.

"How dare he?" She asked aloud.

She raised her head with an urgency to pull out of the parking lot. She had to get away from the eyes that were undoubtedly still on her. She rummaged through the spilled contents of her pocketbook to look for her keys and noticed a picture in the newspaper staring back at her. She immediately recognized those eyes. There on page B5 of the Patriot News was Granny's obituary. It all made sense. The nonstop calls, Quinton being there. He had needed her. And she was so wrapped up in herself that she wasn't there. That was the first time she could think of that he needed her…and she wasn't there.

Tamra felt like her hands weren't functioning correctly. She fumbled to get the key in the ignition and jerked the gear into drive. The loud ringtone of her cell phone startled her. It was a text message from Dennise.

I tried to tell you…

Chapter 14

If Tamra knew Quinton, she knew exactly where to find him. The black, shining rental car parked on his grandmother's block indicated that she was right. She hadn't been on the street in years. Everything had drastically changed since she was there last. Everything except Granny's house. It was as if the immaculate, brick structure had been plucked from a time capsule and plopped in the absolute center of the block. Time had marched right along around the house. And the years had not been kind to 14th and Berryhill Streets.

Every other house looked like it was leaning on the one next to it to prevent itself from crumbling like stale cookies. Everything from major household appliances to tons of debris littered the nearby porches. Then there was the house that Quinton had grown up in. The small patch of grass that served as a front lawn seemed to be the only greenery as far as Tamra could see. There were small window boxes that held dainty flowers in them. The spear topped wrought iron fence was for safety and show.

"Where are we, Mommy?" Jayla asked the question as if they had landed on a different planet.

"Just stay in the car until I come around and get you."

Tamra exited the car and walked around to the other side, opening the door for Jayla to hop out. She clutched her little hand tightly and walked down the pavement since she had to park a few houses away. Jayla coughed loudly as they walked through a large cloud of marijuana smoke. The three young guys dressed like hip hop ninjas just laughed.

When the front door opened, Tamra immediately recognized Quint's Aunt Gwen. She stepped out on to the stoop and wrapped Tamra up in a big hug. She squealed and gawked at how big Jayla had gotten. Jayla twirled around and sucked up the attention. Aunt Gwen told them to come inside and offered them food. When Tamra refused, she made Jayla a plate anyway saying that there was more food there than the family could eat in a year. Tamra smiled. Even though Granny was gone, her spirit of stuffing every person that walked in the door with food was still very present.

Tamra hugged and spoke to the relatives she recognized and introduced herself to those she didn't. She looked at the pictures that hung on the living room wall. They had been yellowed by time but remained in the same spots. There were pictures of Quint all throughout his life. There were toothless class pictures, various sports pictures and every occasion in between. His life was chronicled on Granny's wall. Tamra's heart broke when she saw the one from the day she and Quint had graduated from West Chester University. Q was kissing Granny on her cheek and she wore a smile wider than the Mississippi River. She was the only mother he had ever known.

The sound of boisterous children pulled Tamra from her thoughts. She turned to find Jayla among the rebel rousers. She started to chastise her and tell her to quiet down but Aunt Gwen playfully shooed them into the basement to play.

"I'm so sorry. She gets so riled up around other kids since she's the only one in the house." Tamra began to apologize.

"Hush, now! What else is a child supposed to do but have fun? Us grown folks would be happier if we had some fun right 'long with 'em! Besides, you know Granny loved having kids. Shame you didn't bring yours over more often." Aunt Gwen was trying to making Tamra feel bad and it had worked. "Manny is upstairs in his room." Aunt Gwen was giving her a way out of her guilt. Tamra went upstairs as fast as she could.

She stood with her hand on the doorknob of Quint's childhood bedroom door for a few moments. She waited to see if she could hear anything. And she waited to try to find the right words to say to him. She heard nothing. She thought of nothing to say. So she turned the knob slowly and pushed the door open. It creaked a little. Quint was sitting on the edge of his old twin bed looking dazed and confused. He didn't acknowledge that Tamra had entered the room and she waited for him to say something. He was quiet and held a tattered baseball in his hands. Tamra stood behind him on the opposite side of the bed.

"For as long as I can remember I wanted to get away from here." He broke the silence. "I always said I'd come back for her. I said I'd take care of her like she took care of me. I let her down, Tam. I let her die here alone."

"Oh, Honey," was all she could muster. She walked around the bed and gently rubbed his head. He caved under her touch. He broke down and sobbed. He dropped the baseball. It landed right on her pinky toe before it rolled under the bed. She bit her lip and tried to hide the pain from him. She pulled his head into her body and let him cry. She didn't know what to say. Besides, he probably just needed her to be there, anyway.

Tamra sat on Quint's knee and rested her head upon his. She rubbed his back and let his tears soak her shirt. She had never seen him like this. For the first time, she couldn't fix it for him.

"I'm here, Q," she reassured him.

She laid gentle kisses on the top of his head. He loosened his embrace and cleared the wetness from his face with one swipe of his massive hand. He exhaled deeply and looked at her. Confused, Tamra looked at the door to see if someone had come in behind her. Then she realized he was trying to regain his composure.

"Don't do that," she instructed. He looked as if he was about to ask her what she was talking about. She continued before he could get a word out. "Don't pretend. If you're hurting, allow yourself to hurt." His shoulders dropped even further.

"It's just that, I feel like there's so much more I could have done." He sounded so disappointed in himself. "I was so busy chasing money that I lost time I can never get back. I wanted to be Superman. I wanted to save her." His eyes dropped from Tamra's face to their feet. She got the feeling that he wasn't only talking about Granny.

"She never needed you to save her. She needed you to be successful. Do something with your life. She stayed here so you wouldn't have to. Even Superman was Clark Kent some time, Q."

She kissed his forehead; then his cheek. He instinctively turned and kissed her lips. She closed her eyes and kissed him back. His embrace tightened and he massaged her back. She moaned and he pulled his hands away quickly.

"I'm so sorry," he apologized. "Did I hurt you?"

"That was a good moan. You can't tell the difference?" She teased him to lighten his obvious concern.

He smiled and gave her a few pecks on the lips. Then he began to kiss on her neck. She angled her head to give him full access to it. He nibbled on her ear and whispered softly into it.

"Why didn't you answer my calls?"

Tamra pulled away and looked at him in his eyes.

"What?"

"Why didn't you answer my calls?"

"I thought you wanted to talk about me leaving Chicago." She was honest and to the point.

"So what if I did? You don't think you owed me some type of explanation?" He was killing the moment.

"No, Quinton. In fact, I didn't. Hence the reason I didn't give you one."

She stood up and took a step away from him. He gently grabbed her wrist and guided her to sit down on the bed next to him. She sighed heavily to remove some of the attitude from her voice. She placed her hand on the inside of his thigh and leaned into him. He caressed her arm. She continued talking.

"I know you needed me. And I know you wanted me to tell you why I left the way I did. But, you also know how I am, Q."

"I do know how you are, Tam. And at the end of the day, you're always there when I need you. So it's water under the bride. Okay?"

"Okay." She was relieved. He was letting her off the hook once again.

There was a light rap at the door and Aunt Gwen peeked in the door.

"Everything all right in here? I'm just making sure everything's all right in here." She said it with a suspicious tone. Tamra and Quinton both chuckled.

"Aunt Gwen, I'm almost forty. I'm not allowed to sit in my room with the door closed?"

"I said I was just making sure everything's all right." Tamra was tickled at her attempt to snoop and intrigued by the fact that Aunt Gwen had lived in Harrisburg, Pennsylvania all her life and had a southern accent like she lived in the heart of Alabama.

"Everything is fine, Auntie."

She pulled the door shut but made sure to leave it open just a crack.

"Maybe we should head downstairs," Tamra got up and walked toward the door.

"Hey," Quint called behind her.

She turned and looked at his tall, muscular frame taking up much of the twin bed. She instantly smiled at the sight of him. How manly he was. How much he had grown in their years as friends. It seemed that his mental maturity was now overshadowing his physical changes she had witnessed over decades of knowing him. Tamra was proud of the man he had become. And she was upset because she couldn't be the woman he finally wanted her to be. She raised her eyebrows to see what he wanted.

"You gonna be my Lois Lane?" He asked.

"Haven't I always been?" She replied.

His signature smile flashed for the first time that day and brought her comfort. They headed down the steps holding hands. Her phone vibrated in her clip and she pulled it out to see who it was. It was a text from Elijah. *I can't wait to see you tomorrow.* She closed it before Quinton could see it over her shoulder and shoved her phone back in the holster.

"Is everything okay," he asked.

"Oh, yeah. I'm fine." Tamra lied.

Chapter 15

The next morning Tamra rose early, excited to get to church. It seemed like ages since she had been there. Jayla was just as excited as she was to get there. They both got dressed and out the door on time. Tamra knew it was going to be a good day. They got into the car and Jayla climbed between the two front seats to skip through the songs on the CD.

"Jayla Jordan! Sit down and buckle your seatbelt right now!" Tamra slammed on the brakes.

"I want to hear Come Let Us Worship!"

Tamra rolled her eyes and skipped to track 2 of the "God of Israel" CD. That was Jayla's favorite song and they played it in the car so much that it now skipped a bit. Now, they liked to listen to it just to see how far into the song they could get before it sounded like the choir had the hiccups. Just before Larry Colbert got to the Spanish part, the song went haywire. Jayla giggled and Tamra hit forward on the dashboard.

When they got to church, Tamra went straight to the seat they normally sat in. There was a gift bag in her regular spot. When she went to slide it over, she noticed that her name was on the tag. She wrinkled her brow and peeked inside. Her heart skipped a beat when she saw the top of two boxes. She pulled out the Barbie and Ken dolls and laughed to herself. Jayla spotted the toys and reached for them.

"Are these for me?" She squealed.

"Put those away," Tamra shushed her as members turned and looked at them.

"Mommy, are they mine?"

Tamra shoved them back in the bag and looked in Elijah's direction. He winked. She melted. Pastor Givens stepped up to the pulpit and asked that the choir come and give an A and B selection. The choir had finished the first song and began singing the second one and Tamra was completely wrapped up in a praise that she desperately needed. She closed her eyes, raised her hands and let the presence of God envelop her.

The choir began to sing "Total Praise." She forgot about all the turmoil in her life. She disregarded the sadness that seemed to always be lingering. She threw herself full force into the action of the title of the song. By the time the singers sang rounds of Amen in three part harmony, tears streamed from her eyes and she let them.

"Uncle Q!!!!"

Jayla's voice pierced the air. Tamra heard it over the thunderous drums and the organ. It outdid the combined voices of the choir. And what she said pulled Tamra right from her praise. She opened her eyes and saw Quint holding Jayla in his arms with her hugging his neck like her life depended on it. No one in the congregation seemed to notice. But, Elijah's eyes were locked intently on the three of them. He looked away quickly and Tamra thought she saw his eyes well up. Her heart sank. Quint put his free arm around Tam and hugged her. She sat down on the pew and looked away from Elijah's devastated glare. She, in turn, made eye contact with Tawonda. She had seen the whole encounter and it seemed to bring her sheer delight. Tamra's heart sank even further.

After service was over, Tamra gathered her things and wanted to head out the door. Elijah made a bee line for her. She turned to exit the pew and was face to face with him.

"Hello, Sister Jordan. How are you?"

"Elder McCall," she nodded.

Elijah turned his attention to Quinton. He reached his hand out to him.

"Hello, Sir. I've heard so much about you. I'm so glad you joined us today."

"I was glad to be here. I enjoyed myself."

"You're daughter looks just like you," Elijah said to Quint.

"Why, thank you so much." Quint grabbed Jayla's hand. "I didn't catch your name."

"Mommy, can we go to Mom-Mom and Pop-Pop's?" Jayla interrupted. Tamra couldn't have been happier.

"We really should be going. Have a great afternoon, Elder."

Tamra slid past Elijah and walked up the middle aisle with Jayla and Quint close behind her.

"God bless you guys," she heard Elijah call after them.

"Same to you, my man," Quint replied over his shoulder.

Jayla slipped one hand in Tamra's and the other in Quint's and they skipped out the sanctuary doors. Tamra didn't have the heart to turn around to see if Elijah was watching. When they got outside, Tamra shot Q a look that needed no explanation. He just raised his eyebrows and smiled. She got in the driver's seat of her car and Quint automatically got in the passenger side after helping Jayla in the back. Tamra shot him another look. He gave her the same reply again.

"Why did you say thank you? And what are you doing here?" She spoke through clenched teeth.

"Ain'tnobody thinking about that man, Tamra. And what's wrong with me being here?"

Tamra looked in the rearview mirror and saw that Jayla was totally engrossed in her DS. She continued talking.

"Where's your car? Do you want me to drive you to it or something?"

"We're going to Mom-Mom and Pop-Pop's, right Jayla?" He spoke loudly to get her attention.

"You're coming with us, Uncle Q? Yes!"

"That's up to Mommy."

They both looked at Tamra and waited for her to respond. She just turned the car on and started driving. When they got to her parents' house, Tamra climbed the steps of the house she grew up in and was greeted at the front door by her father. He was overjoyed when Tamra and Jayla came to visit. But, Tam thought he'd faint from excitement when he saw Quinton with them.

"What a pleasant surprise!"

His voice boomed. He kissed Tamra then picked Jayla up and let her plant kisses all over his chubby face. He and Quint wrapped each other in a tight embrace with Jayla smashed between the two of them. She wriggled and laughed as they squeezed her.

"You guys are so silly. Where's Mom?" Tamra walked straight into the dining room sure she would find her mother there. She was right. She had arts and crafts scattered all over the dining room table.

"Who is that with you?" She craned her neck to try to see, not realizing that Tamra had leaned in to greet her with a kiss.

"That's Quinton Davis, Mama."

"Quinton Davis?" She whispered in an octave three times higher than her normal one. "What is he doing here with you?"

Before Tamra had a chance to give her an explanation, the three of them walked in the room. Tamra was glad because she really didn't have one to offer.

"Mrs. Baker, I tell ya. You get more beautiful every time I see you."

"Well, you need to come around more often. How have you been?" Her mom couldn't hide how flattered she was.

"I'm doing well. I'm just in town for a few days to lay my Granny to rest then I'm headed back out to Chicago. But, I knew I couldn't come to Harrisburg without coming to see you guys."

Tamra's dad ushered Quinton into the living room and Jayla ran off behind them. As soon as they were out of sight, her mom shot her a quizzical look.

"Mom, I saw him yesterday when I went to see the family. And he showed up at church this morning! I'm just as shocked as you are that he's here!"

Her mom patted the chair next to her instructing Tamra to sit down.

"Talk to me, Tam."

"About what, Mom?"

"What's going on with you?" Her tone was full of concern.

Tamra stared at nothing in particular before she answered her. She knew there was no sense in trying to lie to her mom. But, she scanned her brain for the way to say it.

"Joe Joe's an alcoholic and he hit me."

Tamra hadn't planned on being that direct but she couldn't think of any other way to say it. Her mother looked like she had been totally deflated. Her eyes immediately filled with tears. Tamra's mirrored hers.

"You have to leave. You have to leave now." Her voice was steady and unwavering.

"Mom, he left. He hasn't been at the house in days."

"No." Her mom interrupted. Tamra started to defend herself but her mom raised her soft, wrinkled hand to cut her off. "Listen to me and you listen to me good. You and that baby have to get out of there. You can come here." She looked as the decision she had just made was final and sat back in the high backed chair.

"Ma, you're not listening to me. He's gone. It won't happen again. I'm not going to let it."

Her mother slammed her hand down on the table. Pieces of paper and glue sticks rattled across it.

"Damn it, Tamra. Once is enough. And if he did it once he will do it again. Trust me. I know."

"What?" Tamra asked in a panic. "Did Daddy…"

"What type of fool do you take me for, Girl? You think your daddy was the only man I've ever been with? I was beat to a pulp everyday for three years. And every one of those days I thought it wouldn't happen again. You know when it stopped? When I left. Please, Baby. Just come home. We'll come up with a plan." She was pleading with Tamra. Tears spilled down Tamra's face. She hurried and wiped them away when she heard the jolly trio walking into the room.

"Jean, what's going on? What's wrong?"

Her father sensed the tension between the two of them and worry covered him. Her mom pushed away from the table and grabbed his hand to lead him into the kitchen. Oblivious to what was going on, Jayla ran off behind them. Quint lightly rubbed her back and kissed her on the top of her head.

"You okay?"

"I just told her about Joe Joe."

"I figured. You okay?"

She just shook her head. He sat in the chair that her mom had been sitting in. Tamra leaned forward put her knees between his thighs. He cradled her hands in his. They didn't say anything. His thumb rubbed the back of her right hand. He turned the diamond on her engagement ring into the palm of her left hand with his opposite thumb. She let a tear slide down her cheek and onto her skin. Quint rubbed the wetness until it disappeared. The words they spoke through the silence were deafening.

"We'll get you through this, Tam." She shook her head and hoped he was right.

Chapter 16

The days that followed were filled with Quinton and uncertainty. Tamra had done her best to be there for him in any way possible. In a way, she hoped that being with him in the days leading up to it would excuse her from having to go Granny's funeral. The last funeral she had been to was Kya's. Tamra wasn't ready for another. But, she didn't know how to tell him that.

So when the morning of the funeral arrived, Tamra lay in her bed stricken with the grief she wished she could take from him and restrained by her own grief that she didn't want to face. She got Jayla off to school and went back to the house. She went to the closet and dug in the back for her black suit. She removed the plastic from the dry cleaner and laid the skirt and jacket across her bed. She took a deep breath and started to get dressed.

She couldn't find the right shoes she wanted to wear. She tore a hole in her stockings. Time was moving way too fast and Tamra couldn't keep up. And then Quinton called her.

"Are you close?" He sounded like a little boy.

"I'm walking out the door now. I'll see you at the church."

"We're here at the house waiting for you. I want you to ride with me."

She stopped dead in her tracks. She mumbled a response. She turned on her heels and went into the kitchen and poured a glass of water. She popped two Advil and they were half swallowed before she even swigged the lukewarm water.

When she pulled onto the block, Quinton was standing in the doorway of the house nervously looking up and down the street. His shoulders dropped with relief when he saw her car. She got out the car and trotted toward him apologizing for being late.

"Don't worry, Babe. I wouldn't have left without you." She only gave him a half smile back.

Tamra sandwiched Quint's hand inside hers in the limo the entire ride to the church. She ignored the side eyes she caught when they walked into the church together. She was relieved when she saw an empty seat on the end of a pew toward the back of the church. Quint tightened his grip on her hand and pulled her close to him as they walked past the seat as if he read her mind. Tamra was relieved when she saw her sister sitting across the sanctuary. She had asked her to be there in case she had an anxiety attack.

"I can't," she whispered. He knew exactly what she meant.

"You don't have to. Just sit here and I'll be right back."

She watched him as he walked up to the casket. She closed her eyes and lowered her head. Her head began to spin and she breathed away the nauseous feeling. When she smelled his cologne wafting by, she opened her eyes but did not look up. She kept her head down until the casket was closed. Throughout the service, she periodically looked at Quinton to make sure he was okay. He dabbed his eyes with a tissue a few times but didn't break down. She felt like she was taking it worse than he was. But the fact that they were sitting together in the midst of this misery seemed oddly comfortable. Quint and Tamra had always been there for each other. This proved that no matter how many years had gone by or what was going on in their personal lives that would never change.

After the burial, family and friends gathered back at the church for the repast. Tamra found a seat in the corner while Quinton made his rounds hugging and talking to family. She wanted to stay out of the way because so much attention was on him. He was definitely Granny's baby and everyone made extra effort to check on him all throughout the day. He had spent most of the day checking on her.

"You okay?"

"I'll be fine. I just feel a little sick. I haven't eaten today."

Without a word, he whisked away, cut to the front of the food line and returned with a plate piled high with everything on it. The smells of all the foods merged together and raced through her nostrils. She wanted to throw up. She picked at the food and forced herself to swallow a few bites. Quinton had gotten pulled away by someone again. She was relieved when her sister came over to the table.

"Hey, Sis. I gotta get outta here, but I just wanted to make sure you and your hubby were okay."

"Shut up, Dennise," Tamra growled at her. Dennise just laughed at her.

They lowered their voices as they realized Quint was making an announcement.

"I just wanted to thank everyone for coming out to show so much love and respect for my Granny. As you all know, she raised me. And I think she did a pretty good job," he struck a pose and everyone laughed. "But seriously. Granny gave up so much in her life to make mine better and she only wanted what was best for me." His voice started to shake. "She was tired and it was time for her to leave here. But she stayed until she knew I was in good hands." He walked toward Tamra. Dennise stepped out of his way.

"Tamra," he looked her square in her eyes. She tried to anticipate his next statement. He grabbed her hands but she did not move from the chair. "If I've learned anything in life, I've learned what it means to take care of someone. Let me take care of you."

Oh God no, she thought to herself. He got on one knee. There were gasps and sighs throughout the crowd.

"Be with me." She didn't even realize he had slipped her wedding set off her finger and slipped another one on.

"How is he gon' marry someone that's already married?" She heard her sister say. A few people chuckled at her statement. Quinton was planted in front of her searching her eyes for an answer. She got dizzy and everything went black.

Chapter 17

Thanksgiving came and brought a sense of calm with it. Quinton had flown back to Chicago with no answer from Tamra. She had worn the ring on her right hand and taken her wedding set off. Quint said he didn't want to push her and that she could take all the time she needed. She had agreed to fly out on Black Friday and spend the weekend with him. She hoped she'd have an answer for him by then; although, that was contingent upon her making some resolve with her home situation.

Thanksgiving was always a wonderful holiday at the Baker house. Once Tamra, Dennise, and Shaun were grown and moved out, they always came home and spent the night with their parents the night before Thanksgiving and then spent the whole day with them. This year was no exception. Shaun had brought his son, Shaun, Jr. over and Dennise brought Ennis and Eryn. Tamra loved seeing Jayla play with her cousins.

Tamra, Dennise, and their mom were in the kitchen cooking and laughing while the kids were in the dining room alternating between playing board games and fighting like cats and dogs. During one extremely loud round of an argument, Dennise walked into the room to settle the kids down. She sent them out to the front porch to get some bottles of soda. Seconds later, the children came running into the kitchen like a pack of wild animals with Jayla leading the pack. Her eyes were wide as saucers and her smile was as wide as her face.

"Daddy's here! Daddy made it for dinner!"

Tamra's mom dropped the glass she was washing causing water to shoot up in the air like a geyser.

"Gerald!" She called out to her husband in a panic.

Dennise headed for the front door. Tamra instructed the kids to stay in the kitchen with Mom-Mom and she followed behind her sister. By the time she got to the porch, her sister and brother were already there. Dennise cursed at Joe Joe and flung her arms about loudly. Shaun stood close by waiting for Joe Joe to look like he would make a move toward her. Tamra walked out onto the porch and tried to quiet the ruckus.

"Joe Joe, what are you doing here? Why would you come here?"

"Yeah, whatchu here for, Joe Joe?" Dennise chimed in. "You need somebody to hit on?"

Joe Joe looked at Tamra in disbelief as she looked at her sister with the same expression. Joe Joe couldn't believe she had told her family and Tamra couldn't believe that Dennise was running her mouth. Shaun's eyes were locked in on Joe Joe. He waited for him to take another step closer to the porch. The screen door opened and Tamra's dad stepped out slowly.

"All three of you in the house."

He spoke to them as if they were in grade school again. Dennise and Tamra went back in without any hesitation. Shaun didn't move. Her dad spoke again.

"In the house.Now." This time, Shaun obeyed.

Tamra stood in the doorway afraid of what was going to happen next. She felt responsible for this debacle. Nothing in her mind could tell her she wasn't. She watched as Joe Joe started to approach her father. Gerald motioned for him to stop. He did.

"You are not welcome here. It is in your best interest that you leave my property before I kill you with my bare hands." His tone was steady and indicated that he meant every word he said.

Joe Joe looked beyond Gerald at Tamra.

"Tamra, if you want me to leave, I will."

"Tamra don't have no say about this house," her dad barked. "She don't run nothing but her mouth around here. Now I said leave."

She walked out onto the porch and stood on the top step.

"Daddy, let me just talk to him. He will leave. Just give me a minute."

Gerald's eyebrows shot up and he disappeared into the house. She turned to Joe Joe in anger.

"What are you doing here?" She shrieked. "What do you want?"

"Baby, I'm sorry. I needed to see you and Jay Jay. It's Thanksgiving. I've never been away from ya'll on a holiday before. I'm so sorry. For everything."

He walked up onto the steps and she met him half way preventing him from going any further. He extended his hand toward her. She retreated back onto the porch. Then she saw he was handing her something.

"What is that?" She looked at it like it a child looks at vegetables. She was unsure and wouldn't touch it.

"I haven't had a drink in 7 days. This is a Desire Chip. It symbolizes my desire to get clean. I want you to have it."

He looked like he was serious. He looked like he was telling the truth. She had gotten so used to seeing him pissy drunk that seeing him showered and shaved seemed so foreign to her.

Joe Joe extended his hand again. This time she reached out to him. He pressed the medallion into the palm of her hand. He clasped his hands around her one hand.

"I'm going to leave. But, I couldn't go all day today without seeing you and my baby. I really do love you, Tam."

And with that he turned and walked away. Suddenly, the front door swung open. Gerald threw her coat, purse, and cell phone on the porch then slammed and locked the door. She was flabbergasted. She knew better than to knock on the door or call one of her siblings to let her in. She slowly gathered her belongings and walked toward her car. She started to text Dennise to ask her to drop Jayla off when dinner was over but another one came through first.

It sucks spending Thanksgiving alone. I'm thinking of you. Elijah

She rushed to the car so she could call him. He answered on the first ring.

"What on Earth are you doing up here on Thanksgiving?"

"I was hoping that you call me and invite me to have dinner with you. I guess that's not going to happen." He pretended to be hurt.

"I'm on my way," she said.

"I'm here," he replied.

When she got to the hotel, Elijah was standing outside. He hopped into the car as soon as she pulled up.

"Where's the baby?" He looked into the back seat. Tamra just laughed at first.

"She's at my parents'. They are having dinner there. My dad and I had a slight disagreement so I left."

"So I don't get no turkey? That's messed up."

"It's all about you huh, Elijah?" She laughed.

"I'm glad you see it my way, Babe." He patted her on her knee and she laughed again.

They got to the house and she started cooking him a delicious meal. This time, she opted to stay in the kitchen until it was done. She made him a plate with enough food to feed three men and sat it in front of him at the dining room table. He devoured every morsel. They made their way to the living room where they both plopped down on the couch into each other's arms.

"Did you like the Barbies?"

"I love them. Jayla has been begging me to play with them. I don't know how to tell her they're not for her to play with, though."

"Let that baby play with those Barbies. I'll be your Ken."

Elijah ran his hand down the sleeve of her silk shirt and she laid her head on his chest. He kissed her twice on her forehead and she tilted her head so that the third one would land on her lips. They were locked in a deep, passionate kiss. Tamra's eyes were closed. His lips felt like a dream upon hers and she did not want to wake from this feeling. When she did open her eyes, she glanced out the front window and saw Joe Joe staring back at her.

His expression was indescribable. Nothing like she had ever seen before. It sent chills through her. His jaw tightened and fury danced in his eyes. He walked away and disappeared from her view. She immediately experienced a fear she only thought was shown in movies. Tamra had a feeling she had just landed herself a leading role in a real life horror flick.

She didn't get a wink of sleep that night. She kept making sure the doors were locked. She kept making sure the phone worked. She couldn't wait for morning to arrive. When it did, she moved quickly. She dropped clothes off at Dennise's house for Jayla and made her way to the airport.

She wasn't taking this trip to see Quinton. She didn't plan on giving him an answer to his proposal when she got there. She simply needed to get out of Harrisburg. She knew he didn't care why she was coming. He'd welcome her with open arms. And that's just what he did.

Quint scooped Tamra up in a huge hug when they saw each other. He could tell something was wrong with her. She blamed it on being tired. He took her straight to his house and tucked her in the bed.

"I thought you wanted to go shopping." Her eyes were already half closed before her head hit the pillow.

"Those stores will be there tomorrow."

"But the Black Friday deals won't."

"Good night, Tam."

He pulled the curtains shut to block out the shining sun, cut the lights out and pulled the bedroom door shut. Tamra drifted right to sleep. She woke up hours later to Quint creeping into the room to check on her.

"You hungry?"

"I'm starving," she replied.

"I'm going to order Chinese. I'll bring it up to you when it gets here."

"Don't you want to know what I want?"

"I know what you want." He waved her off.

Tamra knew he was talking about food but she wished he could help her with everything else in her life. She had no clue. Life would be so much easier if decisions were as easy as choosing General Tso's chicken. Quinton turned on the television and tossed the remote control to her. He crept back out the bedroom. Tamra flipped through the channels trying to find something to watch. She settled for a movie and snuggled further into the covers.

It didn't take long for Quint to come back into the room with her piping hot food. She sat up and he placed the plate in her lap. He settled on the edge of the bed and watched her for a second before digging into his beef and broccoli.

"Is it good? You need anything?" He was so protective of her.

"I'm fine, thank you."

They ate in silence and he took the dishes down to the kitchen when they were finished. She flipped back through the channels again; looking for something they both could watch when he came back upstairs. She wanted something that would keep the attention of both of them so he wouldn't want to talk. Tamra wasn't ready for that. She found a listing for Chris Rock's "Kill The Messenger" and immediately turned to that channel. That would definitely do the trick.

He climbed in the bed next to her and became engrossed in the television. *It worked.* She laughed along with him to keep it up. By the time Chris Rock walked off the stage, Tamra braced herself for the barrage of questions she was sure to follow.

"You want to watch a movie?"

"If you want to."

"What are you in the mood for," he asked.

"It doesn't matter," she replied.

"Comedy or drama?" He pressed.

"Either one." She just wanted him to pick.

"Oh, I forgot who I was dealing with. Miss Indecisive."

The comment cut her but she didn't dare challenge him on it. If he was looking for an opening to the conversation she was so desperately trying to avoid, she wasn't going to hand it to him. He could tell she wasn't going to pick a movie or acknowledge his comment so he swallowed hard and turned to the first movie he saw on. Neither of them was really watching it.

The next morning, they both woke up refreshed and ready to get out of the house. Tamra was thankful that Quint didn't make her talk about not answering him or why she was wearing the ring he had given her on her right hand. He seemed to be walking on eggshells, scared to push her away and Tamra appreciated that. She knew it was unfair to treat him like that. But, she did it and he accepted it.

They got to Water Tower Placearound 11:30 and it seemed that every item Tamra touched, Quinton bought. He dragged her from store to store with intermittent trips back to the car to unload his armful of bags. He bought shoes and purses and almost a whole new wardrobe for her. And she thought about how much it would cost to fly these bags back home. It almost made her uncomfortable. She kept protesting but he insisted.

"Quinton, seriously. This is too much. I don't need another thing today."

"Tamra, you're not going to buy this stuff for yourself. And you deserve it. Would you just live a little? This money is a drop in the bucket for me."

She wasn't sure why but that last comment upset her. She tried to let it slide but it kept nagging at her. Finally, Quinton ran out of energy and suggested they sit down and have a bite to eat. He chose a quaint, Italian restaurant and he sat very closely to her as they waited for their food. The meal was delicious and the conversation was enjoyable. Tamra was starting to lighten up from earlier. She excused herself and went to the bathroom. When she got back Quinton handed her phone to her.

"Someone is blowing you up. You might want to check this."

Tamra took the phone from him.

"I didn't look at who it was," he continued before she could even ask him if he had.

Just as she turned her phone over and saw that her sister had called her multiple times, she was calling again. Tamra answered the phone and immediately heard panic in Dennise's voice.

"Joe Joe came and took Jayla!" She screamed into the phone. "I tried to stop him. I swear I did. I'm so sorry, Tam." Dennise pleaded for Tamra to believe her.

"Thanks for letting me know. I'll be there as soon as I can." Tamra said it as if her sister had just told her that she had left her headlights on.

"Everything okay?" Quint leaned in and clasped her hands.

"Joe Joe kidnapped Jayla."

For some reason, she smiled when she said it. Quinton threw down a hundred dollar bill and guided her out of the restaurant. They got to his car and he looked at her as if she had just suffered a mental breakdown. She was glad he noticed it. She was certain she was on the brink of doing so.

Chapter 18

Quinton insisted on flying back to Harrisburg with Tamra. She didn't have the time or patience to argue with him. He sensed that she was in no condition to talk so they spent most of the trip back east in silence. He handled flight arrangements, he called and talked to Dennise to get updates on the situation, and with his hand gently placed on the small of her back, Quinton guided Tamra through the unfolding nightmare.

Tamra knew where Joe Joe would be. Without hesitation, Tamra instructed Quinton to take her to York. When they pulled up in front of Ricky's house, Tamra flung the door open and flew toward the front door. She banged on it loudly. It flew open and Joe Joe stood before her.

"What do you want?" His tone was flat and cold.

"You know what I want, Joe Joe!" Tamra screamed like a madwoman. "Where is my baby?"

She began to yell Jayla's name and walk through the house. Joe Joe grabbed her arm and spun her around. Quinton placed his hand on top of Joe Joe's. Neither Tamra nor Joe Joe noticed that he had entered the house until that point. The two men stared at each other for a few seconds. Tamra was frozen waiting for one of them to move next. Suddenly, Jayla ran into the room. She sensed the tension between the three of them and immediately turned and ran back out. Tamra pulled her hand from the web she had created. Fury came over her and she snapped. She turned and glared at Joe Joe.

"How dare you? How dare you try to take her from me? You know she's all I have! Why would you do that?"

"For real, Tamra? She's all you have? I can't tell!" He exclaimed. "You have the house that I pay most of the bills to maintain. You put me out and have Jay Jay living with you. You have your best friend Q here with you right now. And you just had some other man in the house I pay for kissing him in my living room. She's all you have? You got more than me!"

He stepped closer to her with each item he listed that she had. She waited for Quinton to step in and protect her again. He did not move. Tamra's mouth fell open. She waited for some type of rebuttal to come out and came up with nothing. Quint found words instead.

"Tamra, what is he talking about?" His head was low and she suspected his eyes were filling with tears.

"That is irrelevant, right now, Q. That has nothing to do with what he---"

"Tamra, what is he talking about?" He raised his head and his voice.

Tamra turned and walked out of the house. She heard Joe Joe chuckle behind her. She stormed out and pulled the handle on the car door causing the alarm to blare. Quinton was close behind her.

"Are you going to unlock the door, or what?" She snapped.

He pressed the button and the lock popped open. Tamra opened the door and plopped down into the seat. He slammed himself down into the driver seat and revved the engine before speeding off.

He drove a few blocks then pulled over to continue questioning her.

"Who were you kissing, Tam? In your house? Was Jayla there? Who is it?"

Tamra grabbed her purse and jumped out the car. Quinton rolled the window down and yelled out after her. She ignored him and walked into a nearby McDonald's. She went into the bathroom and ran her hands under warm water as she thought about what to do next. She thought about what she was going to say to Quint when she got back in the car. How would she ever explain this? When she finally went outside, she found out that she wouldn't have to tell him anything. He was gone.

She went back into the restaurant to try to sort things out in her head. She had to figure out how she was getting back to Harrisburg. She opened her wallet to buy a soda and realized that all the cash she had taken out to Chicago was still in there. Since Quinton had paid for everything on the shopping spree, she hadn't had to part her purse once. *Thank God*, she thought to herself. She'd probably have to spend all of it on a cab to get her the 23 miles home.

Tamra sat in a corner of the fast food joint and peered out the window as she waited for her cab to show up. She picked at a few fries and then gave up on trying to eat. Her mind was too full. She had no clue how all this had happened.

When she saw the cab pull into the parking lot, she ran outside before they could leave. For some reason, she was relieved when she saw that the cab driver was a woman.

"You're pretty far from home," the woman said.

"I appreciate this," Tamra replied.

"You don't have to appreciate it. Just tip good." She squeezed the steering wheel with her broken in driving gloves and headed for the highway. Once they merged onto I-83N, Tamra realized that the highway number was merely a suggestion of how fast the cabbie should go. She was flying. Tamra grasped at the seatbelt only to find out it had been cut out of the seat. She clutched the edge of her seat for a little safety.

Tamra didn't have time to think about her current debacle. She was too busy praying that the car didn't flip over. When they pulled up, Tamra slipped her a one hundred dollar bill and got out.

"Now, THAT'S appreciation, Sis!" The driver yelled behind her before laying rubber and disappearing off the street.

"Did you catch a cab from York?" Quinton was waiting outside her house and blown away by her decision.

"How else was I going to get home," she jabbed at him.

"This ain't my fault, Tam. No way. No how. This is about you."

"Did you come here to question me, Quinton?" She unlocked the front door and they stood face to face in the foyer.

"Yes, I did."

"Well, I don't have time for it right now."

"Make time, Tamra!" He snapped. "You always run away. Well, you're not running away from this. Not this time. I've known you to be a lot of things. But, I've never known you to be a hoe. What is going on with you? Is that why you wouldn't answer me when I asked you to marry me?" His eyes squinted as if he was trying to focus on who she had become. When she didn't answer him, he continued talking at her.

"First you got married to someone else. Then you had two kids on me. And just when it looks like we are getting somewhere romantically, you pull this? Who is he? Do I know him?"

Tamra looked him directly in his eyes and replied to him as earnestly as she possibly could.

"You can set my bags inside the door and lock the door behind you." She turned and walked away from him and began to sob. She didn't even try to hide it from him. She didn't have the strength to even care at the moment. She went upstairs and lay in her bed. She eventually called Joe Joe and was sent straight to voicemail.

"Joey, can you call or text me back and let me know what time you'll be dropping the baby off tomorrow? I just want to make sure she's home at a decent time so she can get in bed for school on Monday. I hope you all have a good weekend together. Please call me."

She feigned as much cheer as she could. She figured it would be best for Jayla to stay in York for the night. She wasn't in the mood to field her ten million questions and she didn't want to spark a custody debate with Joe Joe. She felt her phone vibrate and braced herself for what Joe Joe had to say. But, it was a text from Elijah. *Come to church with me in Philly tomorrow.*

Tamra didn't necessarily want to see Elijah. She didn't care to see anyone at the moment. But, she agreed to go just to get away.

* * *

"Mom, this is Tamra. Tamra, this is Mom."

"Tamra, I've heard so much about you, Darling. I'm so glad you could join us for service today."

Elijah's mom was so beautiful and wrapped Tamra in a tight and welcoming hug. When she finally let her go, she squeezed Tamra's hand as if she didn't want to let her go. She seemed to know that Tamra needed her presence. Tamra figured that knowing more than they were told was a family trait.

After service, Elijah was making his rounds. There were droves of people telling him how much they missed him and asked him how things were going with his new church. Tamra got tired of following him around and decided to find a seat until he was done. His mom came and sat next to her on the pew. She grabbed Tam's hand and patted it.

"How long ago did you lose your baby?" She patted her hand again.

"Almost seven months," Tamra whispered and nodded her head.

"I remember the seven month mark." Tamra gave her a look that indicated she didn't understand. "Oh, Elijah didn't tell you. I lost one of my babies, too. Except my baby was twenty-one. He was my oldest. Straight A student, never gave me a lick of trouble, and he was taken from me." She stared as she spoke. "I can still see him over on that drum set." The memory made her smile.

"How did he die?" Tamra felt like she was intruding but she wanted to know.

"He went out to celebrate his birthday. I thought he knew better than to drink and drive. He knew he could have called me. He couldn't have called my husband," she laughed. "But, he could have called me."

Tamra could see the pain in her eyes. The guilt she carried was evident. She was saddened by the thought that she, too, would never get over it. It would still hurt years from now just as much as it did the days following her death.

"It never gets better, Sweetheart," Mrs. McCall said as if she read Tamra's mind. "You will forever feel that loss. But, you've got to keep living and you'll keep getting stronger. And before you know it, you'll be able to look back and remember the joy in your baby's life and not the tragedy of her death."

Although Tamra didn't believe that to be true at the moment, she smiled and nodded her head. Maybe Mrs. McCall was right and she'd realize it eventually.

"So, is service always like this down here? I may have to move if it is!" They both broke out into laughter.

"God sure shows up around here. That's for sure. You just let me know if you are thinking about moving down here. I'll save you a spot on the front row with me."

"You moving to Philly without me, Tam?" Elijah said from behind them.

Mrs. McCall excused herself after hugging Tamra and making Elijah promise he would call her as soon as he got back to Harrisburg. He said that he had a stop he needed to make and asked if she was ready to go. She grabbed her purse and Elijah grabbed her hand as they headed for the door.

Tamra jumped in the passenger seat of the car and let him drive. He raced up the expressway and she stomped on the invisible brake.

"You're safe with me, Woman."

"I know," her tone failed to convince either one of them.

Elijah cut off a man in a Lexus truck who flipped him off and laid on the horn. Elijah zipped off the Huntington Park exit. He drove down a few streets and pulled up in front of a barber shop on 6th and Wyoming Avenue. He hopped out and then opened the door for Tamra to exit, too. She reluctantly did.

Chapter 19

The Philadelphia street corner was alive. Things buzzed and whizzed around Tamra and she took it all in like a tourist in Times Square. A group of people standing outside the barbershop were stealthily quiet until they recognized Elijah. They instantly relaxed and she saw the females in the crowd begin to smile.

"Welcome to the hood," Elijah whispered in her ear as he pulled her in to him and walked her up to the group.

"E! What's up, Boy!" One of the guys hugged him and patted him on his back.

"You know what it is, Play Boy," he replied.

Elijah took turns shaking hands and hugging the guys. The two girls waited for their turn. They were all so happy to see him. And they all seemed familiar with each other. So when they finally noticed Tamra standing with Elijah, their iciness immediately reappeared.

"This is Tamra," he nodded in their general direction of the group and their shoulders relaxed again.

Tamra felt so out of place there on the corner. She kept adjusting her clothes and looking at what the other two women had on. She wasn't sure if she should label them as women. They looked too old to be living with their mothers but much younger than her 32 years. They had on skin tight jeans, flat boots that came up to their knees, and matching leather jackets that barely met their belts and showed off their tiny waists. The younger of the two had micros in her hair that hung down past her shoulders and were fire engine red at the ends. The other one had a fade with waves and a line up to make any man inside the barbershop jealous. Tamra instinctively ran her fingers across the top of her braids which were pulled tightly into a bun.

"So, Rev," the younger girl spoke up. "You sick of the country yet? When you coming home?"

"It's not that bad out there, actually. Everyone is real nice. And I enjoy the slower pace."

"I see you making friends with the locals." She shot a dirty look at Tamra.

"Kish, chill," the one with the sharp cut interjected. Then she spoke to Tamra directly. "My apologies. We were all stunned when E...I mean, Reverend McCall left the area. You'll have to forgive her. We all miss our man."

"No worries," Tamra said softly. Elijah spoke to the woman.

"Wow, Gi. Let me find out you have become a street general in two short months."

"You always taught me to recognize an opportunity and seize it. No sense in spending so much time around a wise soul and not learning from them!" She winked and smiled at him. He chuckled like a proud father. Tamra thought the whole exchange was awkward.

"Well, I know it's not the first Sunday," one of the guys cut in. "But, I've got my tithes and offerings. The economy is booming in the hair cutting business."

Everyone but Tamra laughed. She watched as the guy handed Elijah a thick wad of cash.

"Are ya'll alright?" He spoke to the guys first. They assured him that they were. "How about ya'll?" The ladies responded in the same manner. "I'll come check ya'll out when I touch back down. I love ya'll."

"It was very nice meeting you all," Tamra said out of obligation. She was actually quite confused as to what in the world had just occurred.

Elijah ushered her back to the car and swiveled his head back and forth a million times on the way. He did not seem comfortable until they were both in the car and the doors were locked.

"What just happened?" He just laughed a little. She raised her eyebrows and craned her neck toward him and asked the question again without uttering a word.

"Look," he sounded as if he was searching for the right way to tell her something. She turned sideways in the seat and sat back to listen to what it was. "I've always had a knack for words."

"I know you can preach. What does that have to do with what just happened?"

"I didn't say preaching. I said words. I've always had a knack for words," he stressed. "There's a difference. I can stand in front of a congregation of any size and give them hope and lead them to Christ. I can look at people who hate their jobs, their homes, and themselves and give them a reason to keep living. With my words. But, that's because I get my words from God. I haven't always been a preacher in a pulpit, Tam. Sixth and Wyoming Avenue used to be my pulpit. And you just met my old congregation. Those men were my disciples and those ladies were my missionaries. They all sold different things for me and I singlehandedly lured them into a life that none of them want to get out of now. With my words."

"Sold things? What things?" Her eyes darted back and forth. She was confused. "Why are you talking in metaphors?" Her voice was getting higher with her frustration.

"Those dudes sold my drugs and those chicks sold their behinds. And they all brought money back to me."

She waited for him to start laughing. Clearly he had to be joking. Then she waited for him to continue to explain. But, the bluntness of his last statement let Tamra know he had said all he was going to say about it. And that had been more than he wanted to say in the first place.

"You're a drug dealer?" She shrieked. "You're a pimp?" She hollered even louder. She looked around for some way out. Yet, jumping out of a moving car in a city she did not know was not in her best interest. So she put her hands to her head to try to make sense of what she had just heard.

"I used to be."

He was driving like a madman. His calmness was driving Tamra crazy. She had a million questions running through her mind and she intended on getting an answer to each and every one of them.

"If you used to be," she used air quotes. "Why did he just give you all that money? And why were those chicks so overprotective of you? Why would you even take me there? You're a fraud Elijah! That's why you listen to Trey Songz and God only knows how many women at Bible Tabernacle you have cooking you meals. You are no different than any of these other men in the streets. And according to what I just saw, you ARE one of these men in the streets!"

She yelled so loud her ears rang. She felt her face getting hot and her hands flailed all over the place only restrained by her seatbelt. He never turned to look at her. He just kept speeding down Roosevelt Boulevard. He slammed on the brakes and came to a screeching halt in the center lane of the expressway. Cars beeped at him as they narrowly missed colliding into the back them. He put the car in park, put on the hazard lights and turned to face her. Her chest heaved as she tried to catch her breath from yelling at him and anticipate his next move at the same time. She was starting to get afraid. She looked around at the cars swerving to avoid them.

"Look at me," he spoke calmly as if they weren't seconds away from possibly causing a fatal fifteen car pileup. She did as he said. "It's people like you that keep those people out of church. I take the money they give me and keep the doors open to the building that you sit in week after week and ask God for a blessing. You think ministries flourish off of the two dollars church folk put in the basket? Get outta here with that mess. You have to love people where they are, Tam. I don't judge them people back there. That's because I know what they are going through. My own mama ain't come see me when I was out there. She sat on that same front pew you saw her on today and prayed for me. I'm not saying that there's anything wrong with that. I'm just saying that I have a different approach. You read the Bible. Think of all the stories you know about Jesus. Now think about how many of those stories took place inside a church. He was always out amongst the people who needed him. I'm not saying I'm Jesus but, those people need me, Babe. I put them out there. I'm going to love them until I can bring them in."

He put the car in drive and proceeded up the highway. He scanned through the radio channels and stopped when he got to Praise 103.9. He looked intently ahead and didn't say another word for the remainder of the car ride. He didn't need to. He had said enough that would keep Tamra's mind reeling for hours. That man certainly did have a knack for words.

The next words out of Elijah's mouth were when he announced that they had arrived at his house. He got out the car and trotted up the front steps. She followed in stride. He opened the front door and motioned for her to walk in. She shivered because it was colder inside the house than outside. He walked right over to the thermostat and cranked it up. Tamra looked around the bare living room.

"I know there's not a lot here. I'm trying to sell the place and buy something in Harrisburg. But, you know with this market."

"It's a lovely place."

It really was but she felt so uncomfortable. After all he had told her about his past, the only thing she wanted in her immediate future was to get home and away from him. Elijah sensed her discomfort. He hugged her and kissed her on her forehead. She was instantly at ease.

"I'm sorry," he whispered. She nodded her head. "You forgive me?" She nodded her head again.

He kept apologizing and kissing her on the head. She closed her eyes and let the sound of him saying I'm sorry replace the bomb he had dropped on her earlier. She rested her head on his shoulder and gently kissed his neck. He tilted his head toward the ceiling exposing more for her to kiss. She did. She pulled him by his hand to the couch and sat him down. She straddled him and tried to kiss him vigorously while slightly lifting her skirt above her waist. She ground her hips in his lap and began to slip her jacket and shirt off. When she attempted to meet his tongue with hers, he resisted. She pulled back and looked at him puzzled.

"What are you doing?" He asked her as if he really didn't know. "Tam, that's not what it's hitting for with me."

Tamra rolled off of him embarrassed. She slipped her arm back into her shirt and wiped a tear from her face. She turned away from him so he would not see her beginning to cry. He sighed heavily and grabbed her hand. He began to lead her up the steps to his bedroom. She sat on the edge of the bed and waited for his next move. He opened a few drawers and saw that they were all empty.

"I'd give you something to put on but all my clothes are in Harrisburg."

He slowly undressed her and then undressed himself. He nudged her to lay down with him. She let her body sink into the mattress and then into his arms. She couldn't stop more tears from slipping onto the pillow.

"Tamra," she looked at him over her shoulder. "I need you to know that I've done a lot of things wrong in my life. And I promised God that if He gave me something good, I'd do everything right. You are more than good. Let me do this the right way."

He kissed her shoulder and laid his head down.

"Elijah?"

"Yes?"

"Keep talking to me."

He raised his head back up and asked her what she meant.

"Just keep talking until I fall asleep."

This man certainly had a knack for words.

Chapter 20

Elijah gently shook Tamra. She opened her eyes and looked around the room to identify her surroundings.

"What time is it?" She coughed to clear her man voice.

"It's four. I need to get you back so you can make it to work."

She rubbed her eyes and sat up. The thought of calling off crossed her mind. Except, she knew she had to get back to Harrisburg and make sure Joe Joe had taken Jayla to school. She grabbed her clothes off the floor and walked in the direction of the bathroom she had noticed the night before. After checking the expiration date on a bottle of mouthwash on the sink, she rinsed her mouth out, splashed warm water on her face and put her clothes on. Elijah was sitting on the edge of the bed when she walked back in the bedroom.

"You ready?"

"I guess," she replied.

He looked in each room of the house making sure everything was off, before he locked the front door and they headed to the car. It was still dark outside and Tamra fought the urge to turn around and go back in the house and go to sleep. Elijah drove a few minutes before they were at the Turnpike stall taking a ticket from the toll machine. He leaned out the window to grab the ticket and handed it to her. Then he placed his hand on her thigh. She automatically put her hand on top of his.

She knew it was wrong, but Tamra could see herself falling for Elijah. In fact, she felt like she was starting to do just that. He interlocked his fingers with hers and she wondered what it would be like to be able to do that every day. His past scared Tamra. Yet, her own present probably scared him even more. She wasn't sure if a future was even possible for them.

"Why do you want to move to Harrisburg?" She asked him.

"There's this little thing called a church that I'll be taking over as pastor." He laughed as he teased her and she joined him.

"You know what I mean. Why don't you want to stay in Philly? It seems like you have so many people you could help there."

"You've never wanted to just pick up and leave, Tam?" She smirked at the question instead of answering. She knew it was rhetorical and she had never wanted to pick up and leave more than now. He continued talking. "We don't trust God enough. I know that He led me to Harrisburg. I wasn't sure why He wanted me to go, but I knew I should go. Plus, look what He had waiting for me when I got there." He squeezed her leg. "Besides, how can I encourage my Philly folks to leave what they know for something much greater if I was too scared to do it myself?"

"Would you ever go back?"

"The way things are looking, I'll be in Harrisburg for quite a while."

He smiled then turned his attention to the road. Tamra looked out the window unsure of how his answer made her feel. She closed her eyes to think about it, but drifted off to sleep instead.

When she opened her eyes, they were in her driveway and Elijah was looking at her longingly.

"We're home," he said softly.

She liked the sound of that. She invited him in while she got dressed and told him she would drop him off at his hotel on her way to work. He followed her to the bedroom and watched her as she pulled an outfit out of the closet to wear. She gave him the remote control before taking her clothes into the bathroom to take a shower. Part of her wished he would follow her. He didn't. She turned the steaming hot water on and let it hit her skin. She threw her head back and imagined. Tamra would respect Elijah's wishes to do things the right way. Though, he couldn't stop her from thinking about being with him now. And that's what she did. When she finally turned the shower off, she hoped the real experience would be as great as the thoughts she had just conjured.

As she cracked the door open to walk back into the bedroom, she noticed that the television was not on. She wondered if he had gone down to the kitchen. Her curiosity was soon quelled, though. She saw her journal that she kept in the nightstand drawer laying on the bed. On top of it, there was a scribbled note from him.

I'm catching feelings so I figured I should catch a cab.

Tamra drove to work fuming. She started to call him and ask him why he would leave like that. She thought about how easy it would have been for a man of many words to just have told her instead of leaving her a piece of paper like a prostitute. *Maybe that's what he taught his girls to do.* Then she thought about Quinton and her heart sank. Now she knew exactly how he felt when she had left him in Chicago.

When she got to work, she got an email from Megan that was sent late the night before asking her to sit in on an interview that was scheduled for that morning. Megan said she was sick and could not make it in. Tamra copied down the information for the interview and answered emails and voicemail messages until it was time to head to the conference room. She was the first one to get there and she waited a few minutes before one of the other managers walked in.

"Good morning, Tamra! Thank you so much for filling in for Megan," Dina said. "I'm sorry I don't have an extra packet available for you with the candidate's information but I'll share with you." The other managers walked into the room. "I would make you a copy of mine but I think she's here."

The door opened and in walked Tawonda.

"Good morning, Miss Barnes!" Dina greeted Tawonda.

"Good morning! Thank you so much for meeting with me today." Tawonda had her best professional voice on. She took her time to acknowledge everyone in the room and then her eyes fell on Tamra. Tawonda was immediately rattled and didn't know how to respond to the sight of Tamra. Tamra was just shocked that Tawonda would even be there.

"Miss Barnes, I know that you are not familiar with Tamra," Dina said. However, she is filling in for Megan, whom you met with previously. Also, Tamra will more than likely be your trainer for six weeks before you are put out on the floor." Tamra's stomach did flips. The look on Tawonda's face indicated hers was doing the same.

"It's nice to meet you, Sister… uh Tamra."

Tamra gave no verbal response and hoped that the managers did not notice the tension between the two of them. Tamra really didn't have a problem with Tawonda. She was over the downright despicable comment she had made about Kya. Still, the fact that she had gotten caught trying to apply for a job after she knew Tamra worked there made her think she should at least keep an eye on her.

The interview was an absolute disaster. Tawonda tried to keep her composure, but it was clear that she couldn't focus with Tamra in the room. They both made a conscious effort not to make eye contact with each other. It still didn't work. The managers took turns asking her questions and she answered them as best she could. Then it was Tamra's turn.

"Tamra," Dina said. "As Miss Barnes' potential trainer, do you have any questions for her?"

This was Tamra's chance to grill her. She could really lay into her and seal her fate by guaranteeing that she wouldn't get the job. Tamra thanked Dina for the opportunity and looked Tawonda in her eyes.

"Miss Barnes, I don't have any questions for you but I wish you luck and I look forward to working with you in the future." Tawonda stuttered a thank you.

Tamra saw the managers gathering their paperwork so she swiped her notebook and quickly walked out of the conference room. She tossed the paper on her desk and headed for the door. She went to the area around the corner where the smokers stood to bum a cigarette off of someone. Tamra wasn't a smoker. She had a few in college; but was never into smelling like an ashtray. Although, the way she felt at the moment, she could be mistaken for a chimney if she had a pack on her. She turned the corner and startled a young girl who worked in accounting.

"Do you have one I can borrow?"

"I, uh, don't smoke often." The girl fumbled with the pack and her hands shook as she handed a cigarette and a lighter.

"I really don't care, honestly. I'm just stressed and I need one. Thank you."

Tamra lit it and took a long drag on the cigarette and then almost coughed up a lung as she exhaled. She smoked it all the way down to the filter. She flicked the butt into the parking lot and walked back toward the front door of the building. She got to the door and heard her name. She turned around and was face to face with Joe Joe.

"Hey," he said.

"Hey," she replied unsure.

"Can we talk?"

"Sure. I have a minute." Tamra looked around nervously.

"I know it's a lot to ask. But, I need more than a minute. Can you take an early lunch?"

"Let me run upstairs and get my things." He smiled and nodded.

Tamra went up to her desk and grabbed her purse and coat that she had failed to get when she went on her search for a nicotine fix. She told her coworker that she would be gone for a while and went back downstairs. As she walked through the double doors, she hesitated before going outside. She was shocked to see how good Joe Joe looked. She hadn't seen him like that in months. His face was full and his hair was cut. He looked rested and at peace. Joe Joe looked sober. Tamra had almost forgotten what that looked like on him. She got into his car and he pulled off down Route 22.

"So what do you want to talk about?"

"I just want to talk to you, Tam. My mind is clear and I'll remember this conversation." He laughed a little.

"Okay." She was hesitant but open to what he had to say.

"So, how's Jayla been?"

"She's good. All things considered."

"Yeah. We were talking a little yesterday and it just seems like I've missed so much in a few months. She is such a little lady."

"I know."

Joe Joe nodded his head, as it was obvious that Tamra was being guarded. He drove toward downtown Harrisburg and found a parking spot near the River Front. They both got out the car and waited for traffic to whiz by on Front Street so they could cross. Tamra flipped the collar of her coat up as the early December wind whipped around her. She stuffed her hands in her pockets and let Joe Joe put his arm around her shoulders to guide her across the street.

"Do you know why I brought you here?"

"No," she shook her head vigorously and looked at him like he was crazy.

"You'll see."

He kept his arm around her trying to shield her from the cold. She fit. She didn't allow herself to get caught up in the comfort she was feeling. She had felt that comfortable feeling with three different men in a short time span. And quite honestly, she was getting tired of her heart volleying back and forth. Joe Joe interrupted her thoughts.

"It was right about here." He stopped and looked out over the river. "We were standing in this very spot when I realized you were the one. We had come to the Kipona because you had to have some funnel cake. You were standing here and you had powdered sugar everywhere. It was all over your face, down the front of your shirt, on your fingers. You were a mess. It was in that moment that I realized you were the most beautiful woman I'd ever seen. I didn't want to imagine my life without you. We were so young. We had so much to look forward to. Now, I knew I didn't make a lot of money and I knew that there were more successful men out there. But, Tamra, my goal in life was to marry you and have a family with you and spend the rest of my life with you. You made me the most successful man in this world. I ruined it. Nevertheless, I swear to God I will spend the rest of my natural life proving to you that I can be the man you fell in love with."

He didn't lean in for a dramatic kiss. He didn't even embrace her tighter. He simply stood there and stared at the still water of the Susquehanna. Tamra stood next to him and did the same. She was so torn. Joe Joe had just said all the things she had been waiting to hear since his alcoholism turned their relationship upside down. She had prayed that God would bring him back to her. And here he was standing in front of her vowing to be all that she wanted and she was wondering if it was too late. Her cell phone rang pulling her from her trance. It was Quinton and without thinking she answered it.

"Hey, you," he crooned into the phone.

"Hey, yourself," she didn't return the tone.

"I didn't want anything. I figured you were out to lunch so I just wanted to call and say hi. Call me tonight so we can talk, okay?"

"Okay."

Joe Joe turned and walked back toward the car. They rode back to Tamra's job in deep thought and silence. He only asked her if she wanted to stop and get anything to eat before she went back to work. She declined. He pulled into the parking lot and parked in a spot instead of pulling up to the front door.

"Tam, I really want you to know how sorry I am. I should have protected you. Not hurt you. It will take some time. But, please just give me a chance."

She reached over and clasped his hand. It was clammy like their wedding day.

"Thank you, Joey." She slipped her hand away from his and got out of the car. She walked to the door of her office and turned and looked at him one time before going in. She couldn't help but smile. God had brought Joe Joe back to her. Now she had to find the old Tamra who wanted him in the first place.

Chapter 21

Later that night, Dennise called Tam. She made small talk at first but Tamra could tell something was on Dennise's mind.

"Put the kids in the car and come on over, Nise."

Tamra's tone indicated that she knew her sister needed her. Dennise's sigh proved that she was thankful for her understanding. A little while later, the kids were playing Wii and Tamra and Dennise were standing in the kitchen whispering.

"So what's going on?"

"Girl, I think he's messing with his other baby's mom again." Dennise didn't even hesitate before spilling her guts. "She had the nerve to call my phone, Tam. She asked me if I knew where he was. Then she proceeds to tell me that he had just left her house and didn't take a shower after they were done…" Tamra put her hand up to prevent Dennise from cursing. She rolled her eyes. "He just makes me so sick. I don't understand why he can't get his crap together! If he thinks he's going to keep bouncing back and forth between us and I'm going to take it, he is sadly mistaken."

Tamra motioned for her to lower her voice so the kids wouldn't hear her. She hated to see her sister upset. She knew Dennise deserved so much better than the likes of Eric but she wouldn't dare tell her that. She grabbed a bag of chips out of the cabinet and crunched one loudly before offering her sister some. She chose those few moments to choose her words wisely.

"You know how men are, Girl. Just know that whatever you need, I'm here for you and I support your decision either way."

"No you don't, Liar!"

Tamra laughed at her sister's comment but she knew she was right. Tamra, in fact, did not support her decision to stay with a man who treated her so horribly. But after telling her a million times, she was done having the conversation. They heard a cell phone buzz and they both looked in the direction of it to see whose it was. It was Dennise's. She looked at the screen and rolled her eyes. Tamra saw a flash of anger.

"Sis, can the kids stay here for a few minutes. I want to go get gas because I'm on empty but I don't want them in the car cold."

"We ain'tgoinnowhere. And I'd like to see you try to get them off that game. Call me when you're on your way back and I'll have them put their coats on." Tamra thought to herself how that excuse made absolutely no sense at all and she knew that Dennise would ride past five gas stations on her way to wherever she was going with no intention of stopping at any of them.

By nine o'clock, there was no word from Dennise, the kids were tired and Tamra was pissed. She found some pajamas for them to put on and laid them down. They were sleep before their heads hit the pillows. Tamra climbed in bed herself and thought about calling her sister to see where she was. But, she knew that would be an exercise in futility. Dennise could be so immature sometimes. Tamra figured she probably had planned to leave the kids there the whole time.

"She's probably getting high. Just wait until I talk to her," Tamra said aloud.

Tamra turned the television on and grabbed her cell phone. She said she would call Quint so she decided to make good on her promise. She scrolled through her recent calls and hit the number and continued flipping through the channels to find something to watch.

"I was just thinking about you, Beautiful."

"Elijah?"

"Don't sound so disappointed." Clearly, his feelings were hurt. Tamra looked at her phone and realized she had accidentally called Elijah instead of Quinton.

"Oh, I'm so sorry," she tried to recover. "I was trying to call my sister; although, I'm always happy to talk to you."

"The pleasure is all mine, baby girl."

Tamra smiled and snuggled further into her bed. Elijah asked her how her day was after he had left that morning. She opted not to tell him that Joe Joe showed up at her job. Then she remembered she was mad at him for leaving in the first place.

"Why did you leave like that, by the way?"

"Didn't you get my note," he asked.

"Yes but, why didn't you just wait for me to come out the shower?"

"Okay… I tried to make the note as plain as possible but maybe you didn't understand."

He was talking to her as if she was an idiot. Tamra copped an immediate attitude. Just before she was about to let him know about himself, her other line clicked. Assuming it was Dennise, Tamra answered it with an attitude. Part of it was for Dennise and part of it was for Elijah. But it was Eric on the line. He was hysterical. Tamra could hear sirens in the background and he sounded like he was running. She heard that Elijah had disconnected their call. He was probably upset that she didn't ask him to hold on. But she didn't have time for a grown man throwing a hissy fit at the moment. She had to figure out what was going on.

"Eric! What is going on?" Tamra yelled at the top of her lungs as she sprang from her bed. She could hear him sobbing.

"She stabbed her! She stabbed Dennise!"

A wave of dizziness hit Tamra and she sat down on the edge of her bed. She couldn't say a word.

"Oh my God, Tam. I'm so sorry! This is all my fault." Eric was screaming into the phone.

"What hospital?" She screamed back. "What hospital?"

"Harrisburg," he sobbed and the phone went dead.

Tamra concentrated to make her hands stop shaking like the wings of a hummingbird. She slowly dialed her brother's phone number. She cleared her throat to pull herself together.

"Hey, Brother. I need a favor," she wasn't doing a good job at disguising her panic.

"What is going on? Is it Joe Joe? I'm going to kill him!"

"Wait, Shaun! NO! It has nothing to do with Joe Joe. I need you to come to my house and watch Jayla, Ennis, and Eryn. Nise's car broke down again so I'm going to go pick her up." She nervously cleared her throat.

"Well, where is she? I'll just go get her."

"Oh, no. That's okay. I'll go get her. Can you come over here? I won't be long."

"What sense does that make, Tam? Why would I come to your house to stay with the kids to have you drive somewhere to get Nise? Just tell me where she is and I'll drop her off at your crib. What's going on?"

Shaun wasn't falling for it and Tamra didn't have the patience to keep up the charade. So she snapped on him.

"Listen, she doesn't want anyone to know where she is, okay? I'm leaving this house with these kids here in 10 minutes. Either you get here or you don't!"

Tamra knew she couldn't tell Shaun the real reason she needed him to come over. He would track Eric down and kill him with his own bare hands. She could tell he was suspicious but he played along and agreed to be there shortly. Tamra paced the floor until he got there and almost wore a hole in her carpet. She called the Harrisburg Hospital and the receptionist, who obviously hated her life, wouldn't give Tamra any information. Tam made a mental note to cuss her out when she got there.

When Shaun got there, she said thank you and flew past him. She hopped in her car as fast as she could and prayed as she raced toward the hospital.

"Dear Heavenly Father, I come to you asking for a special blessing for my sister, Dennise. Dear God, I don't know what is going on, but I know you have her in the palm of your hand. Jesus, please."

Tamra pleaded with God the entire way to the hospital. She found a parking spot and ran to the emergency room doors. As soon as the big black panes departed, she slipped sideways through them. Her eyes scanned the room to try to find someone in medical gear. She had been in the Harrisburg Hospital plenty of times, but her mind didn't seem to be cooperating and she couldn't think clearly. She spotted someone with a name tag on and approached her.

"Excuse me, ma'am. I was told that my sister had been stabbed and was brought here. Can you please help me?"

Tamra figured she would get the woman to help her if she was nice. These people probably saw more than their fair share of frantic people demanding answers in a day. Her tactic seemed to work.

"I'll see what I can do for you. What's her name?"

"Dennise Baker."

"And your name?"

"Tamra Jordan.Baker-Jordan. Jordan is my married name." Tamra didn't know why she felt the need to explain herself. She was so nervous. She began to wring her hands like a wash rag. The lady nodded her head and motioned to Tamra that she would be back.

She found the closest seat available and sat on the edge of it. She looked around at the other people in the waiting room. She knew that each of them had some type of story. Some type of reason they were there on a Monday night. Tamra tapped her foot at the speed of a hummingbird's wings. It seemed like forever before the receptionist returned. She waved to Tamra to tell her to come over to her. The lady lowered her face and peered over the top of her glasses.

"I found your sister," she whispered. "She's going to be okay. Come with me."

The way she talked, Tamra got the feeling that she wasn't supposed to be taking her back to see Dennise. She even wondered if the woman was an actual employee. At this point, Tamra didn't care. She just wanted to get to her sister. The lady punched the button for the double doors to swing open and led Tamra down a few halls lined with curtained triage rooms. She made mental notes of landmarks, so she would be able to find her way back out without drawing any attention to herself. The lady pulled back a curtain and Tamra saw Dennise shifting back and forth in the bed. She winced with pain and then began yelling at the receptionist.

"How long are ya'll going to keep me back here? I'm ready to go!"

The woman ignored Dennise and quickly disappeared. Tamra rushed to her side.

"What happened? Are you okay?" Tamra whispered.

"What are you whispering for? I got stabbed. How did you know I was here, anyway?"

"Eric called me."

"Eric called you," she exclaimed. "Did he tell you I caught him with that tramp?" She shifted again.

"Lower your voice, Dennise." Tamra pleaded and looked around nervously. "What in the world is going on?"

"When I was at your house, Eric's baby's mom called my phone. I didn't answer but checked the message she left and it was of them getting it in. She did it on purpose. So, I went to her house, busted down the door, we got to scrapping and the hoe stabbed me! It's cool, though. She's gonna get hers." Dennise nodded her head as if she had already made up her mind on that. Tamra looked at her in complete disbelief.

"I don't get it, Nise. You're in a relationship with Eric." She stressed his name. "You have kids with Eric. You are being lied to by Err-ric. Why are you mad at her? That's the stupidest thing I've ever heard of. You all are so selfish. And there are children that are relying on you three for some guidance. It's sad. Just sad."

"You got some nerve calling someone selfish, Tamra. You've always been perfect. You had the world handed to you on a silver platter and complained that the platter wasn't shiny enough."

"Oh, please," Tamra rolled her eyes at her.

"I'm real about mine, Sis." Dennise countered. "I have issues. Eric has issues. But, that's who I choose to be with. And if you are going to stop loving me because of the person I can't stop loving then so be it. If you came down here to check on me, I'm fine. Thanks. If you came down here to be your normal condescending self, you can pull that curtain back and get out." Tamra did just that. "And tell one of them nurses to bring me a cup of ice!" Dennise screamed after her.

Chapter 22

Tamra stomped through the hallways of the emergency room and no longer cared who saw her. She was pissed. She couldn't believe that her sister would lie in a hospital bed after being stabbed by her boyfriend's other woman and defend her relationship with him. She didn't ask about her children. She probably didn't even care. Tamra was so upset her burning hot face had dried up tears that normally would have fallen in this situation.

She was still livid when she got home. Shaun's face told of his confusion when she walked through the door without their sister.

"Where's Nise?" He looked behind her knowing she wasn't there.

"You wanna know where Nise is?" Her attitude was flaring. "She's in the hospital. Her dumb behind got into a fight with Eric's other girlfriend and got herself stabbed."

As soon as the words left her tongue she regretted them. She was too upset to censor herself a second before. Now she was wishing she had.

"What did you just say?"

Tamra knew the situation had just instantly gotten much worse. Shaun snatched his coat off the arm of the sofa and walked toward the door.

"Shaun, don't do anything stupid. She's just going to go right back to him anyway!" Tamra knew he hadn't heard her. Her words would have been useless, if he had. She just said a prayer. As she turned around from shutting the door, she heard a set of little feet scurry away from the top of the steps. She shook her head and ran up the stairs to see which one of the kids was up way past their bedtime. She looked in on Eryn and Ennis and they were both sound asleep. She should have known it was Jayla. Tamra pushed her door open and Jayla quickly pulled the covers up over her head.

"Good night, Jay Jay," Tamra said. Jayla pretended to be snoring.

The next morning Tamra called Joe Joe and asked him if he would be able to pick Jayla up from school. He happily agreed. She had a surprisingly productive day at work and had a record low amount of irate calls to field. She hoped that the good news would continue when she went to the hospital to visit Dennise.

When she got there, her sister was just about to be discharged. She cringed before walking into her room when she heard other voices in there. Tamra figured she was giving the nurses a hard time like she did everyone else. To Tamra's surprise, Dennise was being jovial with one of the hospital staff members as they were giving her instructions on how to care for her wounds.

"You're all set, Mrs. Richards," the nurse said.

"Mrs. Richards," Tamra questioned her after the nurse walked out. Dennise sighed and rolled her eyes.

"Yes, Mrs. Richards. As in the wife of Eric Richards."

"Dennise, when did that happen?"

"Over a year ago, Tam. I never told you because I knew you would have something to say about it." Dennise waited for Tamra's disdain. None came. They both were shocked by it.

"Nise, you're grown. And I'm done treating you like you're still my kid sister. Now, if you keep putting yourself in situations like this that will be kind of hard. I don't understand you and Eric. But, I love you. And that's enough. Besides, I have my own crap to deal with."

"Crap? When did you start using such harsh language?" Dennise teased. The both laughed and hugged. "Don't squeeze me too tight. That heifer tried to filet me!" They laughed even harder.

"Let's get you out of here. I know these people are happy to see you go."

"Girl, I'm good. My husband is coming to get me. I'm going to make him wait on me hand and foot! This is all his fault anyway."

Dennise's phone rang and her face lit up. Tamra knew it was Eric. That was verified when Dennise's face looked like it had dropped to the floor. She hung up her cell phone and fought back tears.

"I guess I'll be needing that ride after all. My husband is too drunk to drive."

Tamra bit the inside of her cheek to prevent her from saying anything. She grabbed Dennise's paperwork and wrapped one arm around her shoulders. They didn't speak until they pulled up at Dennise's house. Tamra didn't know what to say. She slid her gear shift into park and her sister got out the car as quickly as she could. She leaned her head into the car just before shutting the door.

"Thanks, Sis. For everything."

When Tamra got home, she called Joe Joe to see what time he would be dropping Jayla off and started to make dinner. They got there within a few minutes. When Tamra opened the door, Jayla pulled Joe Joe in by his hand. He pretended as if he was going to contest coming in. Tamra knew better.

"Why didn't you tell me about your sister?" Joe Joe asked with concern in his voice.

Tamra rolled her eyes. She knew Jayla had heard her talking to Shaun last night. And she had told Jayla a million times to stop repeating Tamra's conversations.

"It's just that it's a family matter. That's all." Tamra said it without even thinking first.

"So I'm not family, now?" His feelings were hurt.

"That's not what I meant." She instantly felt bad. "Would you like to stay for dinner?" She asked as a peace offering.

"If you don't mind. I'd love to."

Dinner was eerily comfortable. The three of them sitting around the dining room table, like old times, made Tamra smile. Still, she knew it would take much more than shrimp pasta and Texas toast to get back to what they used to have. The hour got late and Joe Joe didn't seem in any rush to leave. Tamra didn't want him to. She saw the joy in Jayla's face and was willing to let her enjoy her fantasy as it played out. Joe Joe facilitated the little one's bedtime routine and tucked their daughter into bed. Tamra went into the bedroom. She didn't lock the door. On purpose.

Joe Joe gently pushed the door open and peeked inside.

"Hey," he said softly.

"Hey," she said back.

"Can I come in?"

"I don't care," she replied, unsure of why he had asked.

Joe Joe pushed the door shut behind him and locked it. He sat on the edge of the bed as if it was his first time ever being in the room. He ran his hands along the micro suede duvet.

"You got a new comforter." She nodded. "It's nice. I like it."

"Thanks."

Neither of them was sure what to say to the other. Tamra was waiting for him to say what was obviously on his mind. Joe Joe was waiting for Tamra to show him some sort of acceptance. They both waited for the other. It was like a silent, awkward first slow dance and they were listening to two different songs. Tamra fumbled with the chain around her neck. She couldn't get the clasp undone. Joe Joe walked up behind her.

"Let me help."

She quickly grabbed the engagement ring that was on it and covered it with her hand. She was sure that Joe Joe had seen it earlier but she still felt weird about having him help her take it off. She wasn't even sure why she was still wearing it. Joe Joe dropped the ends of the chain around her hands and she placed the necklace in her jewelry box. He placed his hands on her shoulders and ran his hands up and down her arms. She jumped at his touch.

"I'm sorry." He knew why.

"It's okay."

"You know I love you, right?" She was hoping he wouldn't go there.

"I know you do."

"And I know you still love me."

"I'll always love you, Joey. But..."

"But, what? Tell me this. Why didn't you lock the bedroom door?"

She hadn't locked the door because Jayla wasn't the only one enjoying the fantasy that night. Deep down, she wanted to pretend, too. And she left the door open for him to come in if he wanted to play along.

Tamra turned around and faced him. He wrapped his arms around her and rested his chin on the top of her head. Their breathing slowed down and was soon in unison. They were breathing as one. Earlier in the evening she had hoped he would make love to her. Little did she know, standing in the bedroom in his arms was even better. It was proof that even though she had let another man in her pants, there was still only room for Joe Joe in her heart. They still fit.

After what seemed like forever of hugging, Joe Joe guided Tamra to the bed. He gently pushed her onto the bed. She pulled him down with her. Before she knew it they were passionately making love. She was wrong before. There wasn't a feeling better than this.

Morning seemed to come even faster than she had the night before. Joe Joe and Tamra were only awakened by Jayla pounding on the door. She beat on it like the Harrisburg City S.W.A.T. team. Without thinking, Joe Joe jumped up from the bed and dashed to the door to see what was wrong. Tamra was in close pursuit. He flung the door open and a confused look came over Jayla. She peed right on the floor. Tamra pushed Joe Joe aside and knelt down in front of their daughter. Jayla's eyes darted back and forth between the two of them.

"Jay Jay, what's wrong, Baby?"

"I was going to tell you I had to go to the bathroom but your door was locked and I got scared."

"Why wouldn't you just go to the bath—," Jayla cut her off.

"Daddy, are you moving back home?"

She squealed and jumped into Joe Joe's arms. She didn't seem to be concerned that she was soaking wet with piss. Neither did Joe Joe. Jayla planted kisses all over Joe Joe's face. Tamra pushed them both toward the bathroom.

"Let's get the two of you cleaned up."

"Daddy, what day is it?"

"It's Wednesday. Why? Do you have somewhere you need to be?" He joked.

"Is it the Wednesday close to Christmas," she asked.

"You have one more week for Christmas, Honey."

"Is it close enough to get the tree yet?"

It hadn't dawned on Tamra until that moment that she hadn't even thought about decorating for Christmas. They normally made a big deal about going to pick out a real tree and letting the girls decorate it. Tamra was so caught up in her own drama that she totally forgot about it. In previous years, the tree was half way up before Thanksgiving dinner was digested. Tamra felt so bad.

"If it's okay with Mommy, we can go and get a tree tonight."

Jayla peered over his shoulder and shot her eyebrows up at Tam. She silently asked for permission and Tamra knew it would break her little heart if she said no.

"Of course, we can." Jayla squealed again.

Once everyone was showered and dressed, Tamra noticed that they had a few minutes to spare. The three of sat on the bed and Jayla started to pray out of nowhere. Joe Joe and Tamra lowered their heads and closed their eyes. Tamra's cell phone rang loudly. The ringtone of Total's "Kissing You" clearly indicated that it was Elijah. She opened her eyes and looked to see if Joe Joe had noticed. As soon as Jayla was done praying, he got up and walked out the bedroom. She assumed he did.

Joe Joe offered to take Jayla to school and Tamra called Elijah back as soon as she got in the car. He answered on the first ring.

"Good morning, Elijah!" She was chipper and excited to talk to him.

"Were you busy this morning?"

"No," she was unconvincing. "I woke up late and I forgot to charge my phone last night. I just decided to call you on my way in to work. I have it plugged up in the car." She did a horrible job at lying.

"Oh, that's funny." He sounded as if he didn't find any humor in her story at all, though. "Normally, when your phone is dead, it doesn't ring. Your phone rang twice then I was sent to voicemail."

"I don't know why it did that."

"Oh, okay."

She knew that he knew that she was lying. Elijah didn't seem interested in talking much after that and Tamra was fine with hanging up with him. She didn't want to answer any questions he may throw at her anyway. When she pulled into the parking lot at work, she saw a few people headed into the office with Christmas themed gift bags.

"The Christmas party!" She said out loud.

She had totally forgotten about it. She looked at the clock and mentally tried to pull up who she had received for the Secret Santa exchange. It didn't matter. The liquor store was open by then and she'd go grab something there. She exited the lot and headed to the Wine and Spirits. When she pulled in there, her heart sank. Parked right in the very first handicap spot was Joe Joe's car. In a blind rage, she marched toward the door and flung it open. She yelled his name as her eyes scanned the store looking for him. When they fell upon him, she started telling him off before he had even had a chance to turn all the way around.

"You are such a liar! You fed me all that crap about being sober and I catch you in here? Just leave us alone, Joe Joe. For good!"

She spun on her heels and marched back out the store. She could hear the heavy footsteps of his work books trailing behind her. He put his massive hand on her shoulder to stop her.

"Tam, Baby. Wait."

"What, Joe Joe? What could you possibly say to explain this?" She pointed to the store. Her words spit out like venom from a snake. "What?"

His mouth fell open to explain but he hesitated. She cut him off.

"I knew this was a bad idea." She shook her head and turned her back to him.

"Had you given me one second to explain myself, you would know why I'm here! One of the members of my support group called and I came to talk him out of relapsing."

At that moment, the man that Tamra assumed was the group member walked up and thanked Joe Joe and then apologized to Tamra. She felt so stupid. Joe Joe kept talking.

"You said I needed help and I'm getting it. That's still not good enough. Stop looking for a reason to quit on me!"

His eyes welled up with tears and he jumped in his car, slammed the door, and peeled out of the parking lot. Tamra walked back to her car and drove to work. She thought about what he had said. He was right. For their marriage to even be a shadow of what it once was, they would both have to give everything they had. Joe Joe seemed to be doing his fair share. Now it was her turn. She knew she had to leave Elijah and Quinton alone. She had to give all of herself to Jayla and Joe Joe.

"Lord, give me strength," she prayed aloud.

She parked her car and realized that she still hadn't gotten a gift. And now there was no time to go get one.

"Damn it!" She screamed and hit the steering wheel. "Oh! Sorry, God." She waived her hand in the air toward the sky. She looked in her wallet and saw that she had some cash. She'd stuff it in a company envelope and give it to her Secret Santa. She still didn't even remember who she had.

Chapter 23

Tamra tried to be careful in the days that followed. She was optimistic about her future with Joe Joe but she didn't want to do anything detrimental to Jayla. So she asked him to continue staying at his brother's house. She also demanded that he concentrate on being an active participant in Jayla's life before trying to find his way back into Tamra's bed. He agreed wholeheartedly. She tried to frame her mind to be positive. She wanted to start fresh. But, she and Joe Joe had so much history. So many good memories. Unfortunately, there were bad ones too. Tamra had to figure out how to keep the ones that made her smile and discard the rest.

Tamra and Jayla headed to Christmas Eve service and they were both antsy with anticipation. The holidays had always been a fun time in the Jordan household. And even though things were drastically different than previous years, Tamra vowed to hold on to the tradition of making her baby smile as much as possible the next day.

Everyone seemed to be in the holiday spirit when they got to church that evening. The congregation passed out hugs and well wishes to each person they encountered. Tamra sighed and let her shoulders drop. She loved this place. Elijah seemed to be bitten by the Christmas bug, too. He walked up to Tamra and Jayla with a huge smile and two gifts.

"I feel like it's been forever since I've seen you," he breathed into her ear as he hugged her.

Tamra gritted her teeth to suppress the sensation that was coursing through her. He immediately felt her coldness and pulled away. Jayla excitedly jumped up and down and reached for the neatly wrapped boxes. Tamra pushed her arms down.

"That was very nice of you, but I can't accept this."

For the first time in two months, she saw something in Elijah's eyes that she didn't think was possible. Anger.

"We need to talk. Now." He turned and walked outside. Tamra told Jayla to sit down and then she followed him. He opened the front door of the church and a gust of wind blew in. Tamra wasn't sure if it was from the winter or from Elijah. He nodded as he held the door for some more parishioners to walk in. Then he nodded toward Tamra for her to exit. She did.

"And exactly why can't you accept this? You don't even know what it is. Is it because of my people in Philly? I told you, that's not me anymore, Tam."

"This has nothing to do with your people in Philly. This has everything to do with my family. I told you when I met you that I was married. I just think that it's best for me to focus on saving my marriage."

She started to say she was sorry, but the fact was, Tamra didn't feel she needed to apologize. She was making the decision she felt was appropriate. Elijah didn't respond. He opened the door of the church and walked in without holding it open for her. Another gust of wind blew and almost knocked her down the steps.

Service started and Pastor Givens called Elijah to the microphone to make an important announcement. Tamra figured the church was ready in Reading and he would be leaving soon. The thought of that relaxed Tamra a bit. She knew she would still see him, but it would not be as frequent. She knew that would be confirmation that she was doing the right thing by going back to Joe Joe. Elijah stepped to the podium and cleared his throat before speaking.

"I want to say thank you," his voice was low. "You all have rallied around me and supported me in ways that I forgot was possible. God knew I needed you, Church. But, it's time for me to go. I will take the love you all showered me with and pass it along to the souls of Philadelphia who need it. There are people there who need me."

The church members praised God for his willingness to help those in need. However, his words stung Tamra. He wasn't going to Reading. He was going back home. She thought about their car ride and how she asked him why he didn't want to go back. Now that he was, she was so disappointed. After church, everyone lined up and hugged him to say goodbye. She could hear him saying God bless you to each person. Jayla wrapped her arms around his neck, kissed him on his cheek and darted back to her seat. He smiled and then turned to Tamra. She hugged him tightly and he squeezed her back.

"I love you, Tamra." They let go of each other and she walked back to her seat.

Tamra gathered her things and walked out of the church almost in tears. She kept telling herself that this was the right thing to do. For Joe Joe. For Jayla. For herself. She turned the CD player up and dialed Joe Joe's number. She spoke softly so that Jayla wouldn't hear her.

"Hey, what do you think about staying the night so we can all wake up together."

"I think that's the best Christmas present I could ever get."

Joe Joe came over later that evening and they cooked dinner and baked cookies. Jayla scurried off to bed in hopes that Santa would come earlier. Tamra walked over to Christmas tree and plucked a small box from under it. She handed it to Joe Joe.

"It's not much but, I hope you like it."

He nervously unwrapped it and tears freely spilled from his eyes when he saw what was inside.

"Is this what I think it is?" His voice quaked.

"Come home, Joey. Open the locket."

Joe Joe pulled the house key from the box and fumbled with the silver medallion that hung from the key ring. When he saw a copy of the family portrait that hung on their living room wall inside of it, he broke down and cried.

"I lied," he said. Her heart sank. She knew it. "This is the best Christmas gift I could ever get."

Christmas morning was Tamra's turn to cry. Watching Jayla and Joe together filled her with such joy that she was overwhelmed. Kya's noticeable absence was too. The three of them loaded up and went to the cemetery to place a wreath on her headstone. It was the first time they had all gone together, since the day of the funeral. No one spoke at first. But Joe Joe and Tamra both kept sniffling.

"I miss you, Sissie. Tell God I said hi," Jayla's little voice broke the silence and they both lost it.

Tamra felt like they needed that as a family. They had spent the last eight months hiding their grief from each other. They should have been rallying around one another to walk through the valley together. Although it took longer than it should have, Tamra was happy that they were finally moving in the right direction. She wanted that for her family.

On New Year's Eve, Tamra decided to stay home as opposed to going to watch night service. They had a fantastic evening. They played board games and American Idol on the Wii. Jayla was fast asleep long before midnight. Joe Joe picked her up off the couch and bent down a bit so Tamra could kiss her goodnight.

"I'll be right back." He took a kiss for himself.

Tamra cut the television off and went into the kitchen. She pulled out a bottle she had chilling in the refrigerator and got two wine glasses out of the cabinet. Joe Joe walked up behind her and gasped when he saw the bottle.

"Tamra, what are you doing?"

"Joey, it's sparkling cider."

She held the bottle up so he could see the inscription on the front. He immediately relaxed and apologized. They went back into the living room and sat on the couch.

"You want to watch the ball drop," she asked him.

"I just want to watch you." He stared into her eyes.

"Here's to new beginnings," she raised her glass.

"Happy New Year, Baby," he tapped his glass against hers and they both took a sip. "This year is going to be good for us. I can feel it. I'm strong mentally and I'm ready for a sober life. Love from you and Jay Jay is the only intoxication I need." Tamra hoped that was true.

The next morning, Tamra got up and cooked breakfast. After they ate, they all snuggled next to each other on the couch and watched the Mummers Parade. The constant mentions of Philadelphia made her think about Elijah so she got up to clean the kitchen. A few minutes later, Joe Joe walked in the kitchen with her cell phone in his hand. She didn't realize she had left it in the living room.

"Who's Elijah?" He handed her the phone. She hit the keyboard to make the phone light up and saw that there was a text from him.

Happy New Year. I missed you at church last night.

She looked back at Joe Joe. He silently demanded an answer.

"He's the guy you saw me kissing." He looked like he had been punched in the gut.

"Is that why you're going to church? How are we supposed to work on things if you're seeing him nine times a week? Do you even want to work on things between us, Tamra?"

"Joey, wait. You don't understand."

"Make me understand then." He folded his arms and waited for her to reply.

"He's leaving the church. I won't be seeing him anymore. And I wouldn't have asked you to move home if I wasn't sure that this is what I wanted."

She spoke as honestly as she could. His expression let her know he believed her. Her cell phone rang but it wasn't Elijah. It was Quinton. Tamra rolled her eyes with disbelief. Of all times for him to call, he had to choose this moment. Joe Joe waited for her to answer and she decided to do just that and tell Quinton the truth.

"Hello," she braced herself.

"Tamra, Baby! I'm so glad you answered!" Tamra was confused. A woman was calling from Quinton's phone and it took her a second to recognize Aunt Gwen's voice.

"Oh! Hi, Aunt Gwen. How are you?"

"Tamra, Quinton's been in a terrible accident. Is there any way you can come out to Chicago?"

"What?" Tamra shrieked into the phone.

"Yes, Baby. I flew out here first thing this morning. If there's any way you can make it, I suggest that you do so, Honey. Please." Tamra heard a muffled voice in the background and then Aunt Gwen spoke into the phone. "He said he will pay for you to fly out if you need some money."

Tamra couldn't think straight. Joe Joe was clearly alarmed by her demeanor. He stood close to her and waited for her to get off the phone.

"I'll have to see, Aunt Gwen. But, I will do my best."

"Thank you, Baby. Thank you so much." Her voice was heavy laden with concern and stress.

"What's going on?" Joe Joe asked her as soon as she put the phone down.

"Quinton," she said. His face dropped. "He's been in an accident."

Chapter 24

The first words out of Joe Joe's mouth were almost as shocking as the news she had just received on the telephone.

"Go check on him. I trust you. We will be right here when you get back."

Tamra felt like a weight had been lifted off her shoulders. She was genuinely concerned about Quinton and if he was okay. But, things were so fragile with her and Joe Joe and she didn't want to jeopardize what they seemed to be working toward.

Tamra called Aunt Gwen back and made arrangements to fly to Chicago. She scheduled the next flight out and only packed an overnight bag. She would go see if he was okay and come right home. She had never stepped foot in a medical class so her being there didn't really matter. Joe Joe dropped her off at the airport hours later and she got settled in the aisle seat she was lucky enough to snag.

Thoughts raced through her head. She questioned why she was even going. Everything she had been praying to recover was waiting at the other end of the tarmac and she was racing off into the friendly skies to check on Quint.

An ice, cold chill ran through her when she walked into the hospital. She rubbed the small piece of paper that she had written all the information down on between her thumb and pointer fingers. She was surprised the ink hadn't spread all over her hands. She walked up to the nurse's station and asked to be pointed in the direction of Quinton's room number. When she got there, she stood outside for a second and breathed deeply. She was trying to muster up the courage to walk in. One foot in front of the other, she stepped into the room. Aunt Gwen jumped up from the chair and rushed over to her.

"Tamra, I am so glad you came, Sweet Pea," she whispered. "You're the only person he's been asking for."

A nurse trotted into the room and stood closely to them. It made Tamra feel uncomfortable.

"I'm sorry, Ma'am. Only family can see Mr. Davis right now."

"Well, Ma'am," Aunt Gwen said with an attitude. "This is his wife." That made Tamra want to throw up.

The nurse looked like she didn't believe her but didn't want to press the issue so she apologized and backed out of the room. Aunt Gwen took Tamra's bag from her and pushed her around the drawn curtain toward the bed. Quint was scratched all over his face. The slits and sutures on his swollen face made him look like Frankenstein. He tried to smile at the sight of her but grimaced in pain. She walked over to him and placed her hand on top of his.

"Quinton, what happened?"

"Early New Year's celebration," he was weak and barely whispering. She leaned in closer to hear him. "I honestly thought I was okay to drive. I lost control and totaled my whip, Babe. But, I can replace my car. I'm worried about these cuts on my sexy face."

He attempted to laugh and broke into a fit of coughs. Tamra squeezed his free hand. She didn't know what else to do. When he calmed down, he cleared his throat began to speak again. He was unsuccessful so Tamra put the crinkled straw of the nearby water jug to his lips for him to get a drink of water. A drop ran down his chin and she wiped it off for him. He smiled.

"Thank you for coming," he said. "I knew you loved me. And I knew you would come."

"Quinton, I…"

"Just let me get this out. I don't care what it takes. I want to be with you. My offer still stands. I've waited this long. I'll wait forever for you."

"You don't have to wait any longer," she replied. "I'll give you your answer right now."

His eyes danced with excitement. He looked like he would jump out of the bed if he wasn't hooked to various tubes.

"I'm staying with Joe Joe." She was straight and to the point.

"What?" Fury flashed in his eyes now. Aunt Gwen whimpered behind her. "Why the Hell did you even come out here then?" He was devastated.

"Quinton, I do care about you. But, I have to save my marriage. I love him. I'm so sorry."

She pulled the engagement ring he had given her weeks ago out of her pocket and placed it next to his cup of ice water. He turned his head and looked out the window as if he could not bear to look at it. Tamra was overwhelmed with guilt as she knew that this was the moment she had lost one of her best friends. And in true Tamra fashion…she turned to walk away.

When she got to the door, she heard the bedside tray and the contents on top of it go crashing all over the place. She walked to the elevator as quickly as she could but her whole entire existence seemed to be moving in slow motion. She knew she only had a few seconds before she began to sob. She was relieved when she got on the elevator alone. As soon as the doors closed, she slid down wall and bawled her eyes out. She continued to cry until she got to a bathroom in the Harrisburg International Airport early the next morning.

She did her best to disguise her puffy eyes from Joe Joe. But the first look at him and his expression told her that she hadn't done a good job. He was upset. He was short and curt with her on the way home. She soon figured out why.

When she walked onto the porch of the house, there was an enormous bouquet of all white flowers. It was at least twice the size of the first one Elijah had sent her. Tamra's mouth fell open like an old fence hanging on by one rusty hinge. She could not believe it. Joe Joe walked in the house and stood in the foyer waiting for her to come inside. He slammed the door behind her.

"Elijah brought those for you." Of course, she already knew who they were from. "He wanted to say goodbye to you and he had the nerve to leave those here, Tam. You better check him before I do." He walked away from her without another word. She followed behind him.

"Joey, Baby. I will throw them away. There is no reason for me to say anything to him. I'm done. The only person I want to talk to is you. I just want our family back."

She stayed up half of that night thinking about what she had told Joe Joe. She tossed back and forth both in body and in thought. Tamra really did want her family back. On the other hand, she had trained herself to face a new sense of normalcy that did not include Joe Joe. After all the work of getting used to not having him, she wasn't sure if she would be able to accept that he was back. She wondered if having him back was what she really wanted or if it was what she thought she needed. The first thing she did when Joe Joe was out of the house was completely contradictory to her statement to him earlier. She called Elijah.

"Yo," he answered. That threw her off.

"Excuse me?"

"You like those flowers?" He sounded so arrogant and even chuckled a bit.

"Elijah, why would you do that? Why would you come to my house? I told you I was trying to work things out with my husband." He was quiet and didn't respond at first. "Hello," she asked.

"Oh, that wasn't a rhetorical question?" He laughed again. "Look, I always get what I want. And I want you. Tell me you don't feel the same way." Tamra couldn't find any words to dispute his accusation.

"I mean, I care for you, Elijah. But, this is my husband. Wouldn't God want me to be with my husband?"

"Don't give me that holy shit now, Baby Girl." Tamra gasped aloud to hear him curse. "I've been reading you like a self-published debut novel since the day I met you. What did I tell you then? You are not living. When are you going to start to live, Tamra? For you?" Tamra hung up the phone.

She dialed Dr. Steele's office and asked to speak directly to her.

"Mrs. Jordan, how are you?" Her voice was calm and serene.

"I'm fantastic, Dr. Steele. Is there any way you can squeeze me in? I'm ready." The confidence in her voice was almost alarming.

"You sound like it. Are you free this afternoon?"

Tamra walked into Dr. Steele's office later that day feeling like a brand new woman. Her posture was straighter than a prima ballerina and her steps were strong and calculated.

"My goodness, Tamra! It is such a pleasure to see you in such great spirits. Talk to me."

"Well, Doc. I came to say goodbye. I got confirmation from someone about something you said to me. I'm ready to live for me. I can't spend the rest of my life trying to pay restitution on a crime I didn't commit. The guilt trip is over."

Tamra didn't really give her a chance to respond. She hugged her with a genuine and tight embrace and walked out. When she got to the car, she called her parents and siblings and asked if they could come by the house that evening for dinner. She was excited when they all agreed. She pulled her sunglasses from atop her head and headed home to prepare a feast for them. She smiled as the sun shone through the front of her car. Tamra was ready to live.

When her family was settled around the table and they were devouring the meal she had cooked, Shaun stopped mid-bite and looked around.

"Okay. What's this about?" He was suspicious.

Dennise wrinkled her brow. She adjusted her arm that was restrained in a sling. Everyone at the table turned and looked at Tamra.

"Uh, kids? Why don't you all go and play?" Tamra's mom said nervously.

"Aw, man!" Ennis complained. "I was just about to eat my chicken!"

"What did Mom-Mom say, Boy? Go!" Dennise snapped.

The kids all scurried upstairs as everyone looked back at Tamra.

"I love ya'll, but I'm leaving." She waited a few seconds to let them digest their first bite and her news. "I'm moving to get a fresh start. Joe Joe, I'll be in touch about how we will work things out with Jayla."

Joe Joe smirked, obviously thinking that it was a joke. She got up and kissed each person sitting at her dining room table and then ran upstairs to grab the bags she had packed and stowed away in the closet earlier that day. She summoned Jayla and rushed her along. She started to ask Tamra a million questions, but decided against it when she saw that her protests or inquiries would not be tolerated or acknowledged.

"We're taking a trip. We can stop at McDonald's and get you something to eat when we get on the road."

"Oooh! Is Daddy coming?"

"No."

Tamra kept moving. She walked down the steps and out the front door of the house.

"Well damn," was the last thing she heard her brother say as she closed the door behind them. No one had even gotten up from the table.

Tamra drove a few miles and then started dialing on her phone. The call was quickly answered.

"Yo," she echoed his tone from their previous conversation. They both laughed. "I did it. I'm on my way."

After initially hanging up on Elijah earlier that day, Tamra called him back when they both had calmed down. At first, she didn't want to admit that he was right but he was. Tamra had fallen for this man and couldn't explain why she couldn't shake him. Yet one thing she didn't question was whether he loved her back. She knew what life was like in Harrisburg and she probably would get lost within five minutes of arriving in the City of Brotherly Love. Still she hadn't taken a chance on herself in years. Something felt right about starting with him, though. And if it didn't work, that was a decision that Tamra would have to be willing to live with. Either way, Tamra was ready to live.

"Mommy, who was that? Where are we going?" Jayla asked from the back seat.

"Do me a favor and pray, Baby Girl."

She smiled as Jayla started to say the Lord's Prayer. She rolled down her window and leaned out a bit to take the ticket that was sticking out of the toll booth machine.

Tamra was amazed with how far she had come in such a short time. Her journey had taken her places she never imagined she would go. And she knew she would never be able to go back now. She was okay with that. Jayla was safely secured in the back seat and Tamra was excited about the open road ahead of her. She turned the CD player up and accelerated. Her future was waiting and she planned on getting there as fast as she could. She broke out into laughter when she read an oversized green and white road sign. Philadelphia: 90 miles ahead.

<u>Coming</u>

<u>Januaury</u>

2012

"Grey Skies"

Chapter 1 – Precious

"I am so mad right now. I don't even have the words!" Precious spoke to her twins through clenched teeth. They had been fighting over a half of a sip of orange juice and spilled it on her granite, kitchen countertop. The seven year old miniatures of her husband stood frozen by her fury. "Just git." She shooed them out of her way and began to clean up the mess.

"Whatchu fussin' about now?" Adrian wrapped his cut arms around his wife's waste and nestled his nose just behind her right ear. She laughed out loud and turned to fully embrace the love her life. He pecked her on the lips three times, grabbed a piece of bacon from behind Precious, and yelled for the kids to head to the door.

"I love you, Baby." Precious could barely make out what he was saying with his breakfast crammed in his mouth.

"You, too," she stated more to herself than him since he was already throwing his car in reverse to back out of the driveway. Precious rinsed the dishes and stacked them in the sink for the maid to do later. She grabbed her work bag and prepared for her drive to South Street.

Precious went through her daily regimen of opening the salon she co-owned with her sister, Porsche. One second after she turned the answering service off, the phone began to ring. The first four calls were from clients begging to be scheduled for an immediate appointment. The fifth call was from Porsche.

"Grey Skies Salon and Spa. How can I help you?"

"Hey, Girl. Look in my book and see when my first appointment is."

"Uh, please?!?!"

"Bitch, I ain't one of your kids! Am I scheduled for 9 or 10?"

"Luckily, 10," Precious said looking at the clock. "It's already 8:30. Don't have your clients waiting on you." All she heard was the dial tone.

"Oh, Hell no." Precious promptly called her back and finished the regular cuss out that she gave her sister on a weekly basis…and then she hung up on her.

Before long, the shop was filled with beauticians, clients, and the smell of burning hair. Precious was proud of the salon. She and Porsche had been doing hair for as long as she could remember. And they worked hard to move from three dryers and a sink in a basement to the upscale, unisex establishment they were in now.

Grey Skies was known for the best service in Philly. Precious ran the hair salon and Porsche ran the attached all-female employed barbershop. Once she realized that people were looking for a reason to stick around at the shop, Precious gave it to them. She brought in a gourmet chef, a masseuse, and flat screen televisions. If she would've put beds in the back, she could charge rent. She'd often catch someone in the corner dozing off to sleep.

"Just go home, Boo," she'd tell them. "We'll be open tomorrow."

As she began to admire the hard work that was put into the renovated building, she heard her little cousin coming in.

"Hey, Sis! You look fabulous as always!"

"Jamie, why are you talking with a lisp?" She asked him. "And are those fake lashes you have on?" Precious was horrified.

"Don't start, Miss Honey." He snapped and twirled.

"How is my favorite fairy," Porsche asked as she entered the salon from her side of the building.

"Fiiiiiiiiish," he screamed. They shared double air kisses and Precious rolled her eyes. "I need my Mohawk touched up." The two of them disappeared, chattering about the new men in their lives.

Precious didn't take a lot of clients anymore. She stayed so busy doing books and paying bills for both the house and the company that she had to cut her number of clients in half. But, Ms. Shirley was one of her first customers and wouldn't let anyone other than Precious touch her short, silver tresses.

Ms. Shirley took her time and hobbled up the two small steps and headed for Precious' station. She put a cape on the elderly woman and began to walk her to the shampoo room.

Suddenly, the door opened and in strutted a gorgeous, statuesque woman with a sharp, cream suit on and matching Nine West, peep toe heels. She walked straight at Precious, which made her uneasy. The woman pushed her oversized shades up into her beautiful blonde weave exposing a black eye.

"Precious Grey?" She spoke loudly, attracting the attention of everyone that heard her. "I'm your husband's lover and he did *this* to me when I told him I'm leaving," she said pointing to the evidence of the ass whooping' she recently received.

"Ms. Shirley, go ahead to the shampoo bowl. I'll be right in."

Once the lady was out of ear shot, Precious looked her in her eyes and fingered the pair of scissors in her smock.

"What did you say?" she asked flatly.

"You heard me, you dumb bitch. I've been screwing Adrian for two years. I just thought you should know."

Precious felt the Earth skip one whole rotation as her perfect life immediately ended and she fought hard against a sudden wave of nausea. She blinked once and swallowed spit to regain her composure.

"Well, did Adrian tell you I'm a Libra? Precious asked calmly.

"What the fuck does that have to do with anything?" She was confused.

"I believe in balance. So I'm about to make your left eye match your right one."

In one fell swoop, Precious punched the living daylights out of the woman that stood at least four inches taller than her. She sent her crashing backward into a display of bottles of nail polish and they rolled all over the carpet in the waiting area. Precious didn't wait for her to hit the floor before she continued to beat her. With each punch and slam of this complete stranger's head, she released all the anger, frustration, and confusion that had been, until this moment, inexplicably locked in her chest lately.

No one dared to break it up, either. They let her get it all out. She finally got up, pushing down on the woman's abs for leverage, and went and sat in the chair at her station.

Stunned, everyone in the salon was silent. From the back of the room, Ms. Shirley wondered out loud, "Is someone gonna wash my hair?"

Chapter 2 -Porsche

"What the Hell is that?" Porsche grabbed her 9mm hand gun and tucked it in the back of her black hot pants. She kicked off her heels and ran toward the commotion coming from the salon. When she got there, she saw her twin sister walking away from a woman who was clawing at the receptionist's desk, trying to stand up.

Porsche high tailed it to go check on Precious. But, she pushed Beyoncé's reject stunt double back down to the floor first. Porsche rounded the corner and fired off expletive laced questions to figure out what had occurred. But, she quickly saw that her sister was in no condition to answer any questions. So she turned her attention to the clients. They chimed in, one after another, acting the story out. From what Porsche gathered, Precious was clearly the winner. But, from the look in her eyes, she lost everything she ever wanted.

That's her own damn fault, Porsche thought to herself. The only thing Precious and Porsche ever shared was their mother's womb for 7 ½ months. And that was too long for Porsche's liking. So she made moves, sending their mother into early labor. She's been making moves ever since…And it was situations like that that prompted never to get setting with anything in the first place. She changed men like she changed her lace panties and changed her hair more often than that!

Currently, it was jet black and hung to her shoulders in a slanted bob. She stood in the mirror and ran through it until ever strand bowed to the command of her fine toothed comb.

"You gon' be aight, Shawty?" a customer asked walking up behind her.

"Get outta my face before I shoot you." She was dead serious.

Porsche finished edging her last client, pocketed the cash she made throughout the day and exited the building without so much as batting an eyelash at her still distraught twin. She hopped on her customized Ducati sports bike and smiled as the thunderous vibrations rumbled beneath her. She gyrated her hips like she did atop her man plenty of nights, revved the engine, and peeled off. Her tires laid rubber for the first 20 feet. Then she eased off the gas, making sure she left no further traces of where she was going.

Porsche pulled up to her Center City brownstone and backed her bike into the garage. She jumped right into her black, BMW X5 and started punching numbers on the cell phone mounted on the dashboard.

"You on your way," the baritone voice on the other end inquired.

"I'll be there soon."

"Not soon enough. I can't wait to see…"Porsche hung up on him.

Sharif was the closest thing to love that Porsche had ever felt. They met while she was visiting her boyfriend in the Frackville Penitentiary. He was in the visiting room calming the nerves of his emotional and very visibly pregnant baby's mom. Porsche made up in her mind, second after seeing him for the first time that she wanted him. The jailbird she was visiting became pleased and confused when her random appearances became more consistent. And his mounting questions were answered when she walked right past him and into Sharif's arms one day. He was so irate, that the guards had to restrain him and put him into solitary confinement. To show her gratitude, Porsche slipped one of them a fifty dollar bill and her number.

See, Porsche learned early in life that pussy rules the world. And no woman had a better shot than hers. She hated dumb ass women that took the pearl in their pants for granted. Like her sister. *If Precious thought like me she wouldn't even care.* Porsche has only been surprised once to find out that a man was cheating...her dad. And if he could cheat, she was instantly convinced that they all do. *There are no exceptions to the rule.*

Once Porsche removed faith in anyone except the goddess between her legs, she stopped being disappointed.

By the time she walked through the door without knocking first, Sharif was hot.

"Why'd you hang up on me?" She turned around and walked right back to the door.

"Yo yo yo," he shut the door. "Don't leave." Sharif closed in on her and kissed her passionately. His coarse, pointed beard brushed against her chin and felt like someone was feather dusting her face with a Brillo pad.

She felt his hands roam around her voluptuous hips and then to her inner-thigh. He stuck his fingers inside the inseam of her shorts and was met by her heat. She parted her legs to let him enter her and he backed her into the door. She ground her hips and sexed his hand. He pressed hard against her and she could feel his desire through his basketball shorts. She traced the waves in his head with her fingertips and soaked his, trying not to orgasm.

Suddenly, someone banged on the door just on the other side of Porsche's head. Her instinct was to push Sharif to the ground and draw her weapon. Just before she pulled the trigger, Sharif's little brother identified himself. Sharif opened the door and both men noticed the onyx gun her Porsche's hands at the same time.

Sharif hurriedly shut the door and questioned her in a panic.

"What are you doing? You can't have that in here! I'm a felon!"

"*You're* a felon. I'm not. I'm allowed to have it anywhere I want," she said matter-of-factly. She walked to Sharif's bedroom without apologizing for being seconds away from blowing Khalil's head off. She never even said hello.

Once inside the room, she took her clothes off and crawled in the King-sized bed. She was going to finish what Sharif started before they were so rudely interrupted. She moaned...loudly...on purpose. Seconds later she heard the front door slam and lock and Sharif came rushing into the room.

He started to make love to her but, she only fucked him back. He grunted and told her he loved her. With each deep thrust, he tried to reach her heart. She held her breath, closed her eyes and exploded all over him. That was the best she could do.